RISING
WATER

RISING WATER

THE STORY OF THE THAI CAVE RESCUE

MARC ARONSON

atheneum

Atheneum Books for Young Readers

New York London Toronto Sydney New Delhi

ATHENEUM BOOKS FOR YOUNG READERS • An imprint of Simon & Schuster Children's Publishing Division • 1230 Avenue of the Americas, New York, New York 10020 • Text copyright © 2019 by Marc Aronson • Cover photograph copyright © 2018 by Tham Luang Rescue Center via AP Images • Map on p. 11 and diagrams on pp. 42-43, 78-79 copyright © 2019 by Rick Britton • All rights reserved, including the right of reproduction in whole or in part in any form. • ATHENEUM BOOKS FOR YOUNG READERS is a registered trademark of Simon & Schuster, Inc. Atheneum logo is a trademark of Simon & Schuster, Inc. • For information about special discounts for bulk purchases, please contact Simon & Schuster Special Sales at 1-866-506-1949 or business@simonandschuster.com. • The Simon & Schuster Speakers Bureau can bring authors to your live event. For more information or to book an event, contact the Simon & Schuster Speakers Bureau at 1-866-248-3049 or visit our website at www.simonspeakers.com. • Also available in an Atheneum Books for Young Readers hardcover edition • Interior design by Vikki Sheatsley • The text for this book was set in Baskerville MT. • Manufactured in the United States of America • 0320 OFF • First Atheneum Books for Young Readers paperback edition April 2020 • 10 9 8 7 6 5 4 3 2 1 • The Library of Congress has cataloged the hardcover edition as follows: Names: Aronson, Marc, author. • Title: Rising water : the story of the Thai cave rescue / Marc Aronson. • Description: New York : Atheneum Books For Young Readers, an imprint of Simon & Schuster Children's Publishing Division, 2019. • Identifiers: LCCN 2018047593 | ISBN 9781534444133 (hardcover) | ISBN 9781534444140 (pbk.) | ISBN 9781534444157 (eBook) • Subjects: LCSH: Caving—Search and rescue operations—Thailand—Chiang Rai (Province)—Juvenile literature. | Caving accidents—Thailand—Chiang Rai (Province)—Juvenile literature. • Classification: LCC GV200.645 .A76 2019 | DDC 796.52/509593—dc23 • LC record available at https://lccn.loc.gov/2018047593

PHOTOGRAPHY CREDITS
Interior: pages v: AP Photo/Thailand Navy SEALs; 4: iStock; 21: courtesy William Stone; 23: courtesy Ruengrit Changkwanyuen; 24: Krit Phromsakla Na Sakolnakorn/APF/Getty Images; 27: AP Photo/Royal Thai Navy; 29: courtesy Royal Thai Navy; 31: AP Photo/Royal Thai Navy; 45: AP Photo/Sakchai Lalit; 50: courtesy Wang Ke of the Peaceland Foundation; 57: courtesy SWNS; 59: courtesy SWNS; 63: Ye Aung Thu/AFP/Getty Images; 70: courtesy Wang Ke of the Peaceland Foundation; 76: courtesy DVIDS/Captain Jessica Tait; 77: courtesy DVIDS/Captain Jessica Tait; 82: courtesy Thai Navy SEALs; 91: courtesy Wang Ke of the Peaceland Foundation; 103: Vincent Thian/AP; 110: courtesy Rafael Estrada Calvao

Insert: pages 1: iStock; 2: courtesy William Stone; 3 *(top)*: AP Photo/Tassanee Vejpongsa; 3 *(bottom)*: courtesy Thai Navy SEALs; 4 *(top)*: AP Photo/Hathai Techakitteranun/picture-alliance/dpa; 4 *(bottom)*: AP Photo/Kyodo; 5: AP Photo/Tham Luang Rescue Operation Center; 6 *(both)*: courtesy Thai Navy SEALs; 7: courtesy Thai Navy SEALs; 8 *(top)*: courtesy Thai Navy SEALs; 8 *(bottom)*: AP Photo/Kyodo

This book is dedicated to Sergeant Sam, who gave his life, and to all the heroes of the rescue, from the Thai middle school volunteers to the international crew of cave divers. You accomplished the impossible. It is also written to honor the world's undocumented and stateless refugees and migrants—may you all find safe and welcoming homes.

The hands of rescue workers from around the world symbolize the spirit of cooperation that characterized the effort to save Coach Ek and the twelve young soccer players.

CONTENTS

CAST OF CHARACTERS

THAI

Members of the Wild Boars Club (asterisk means trapped in the cave)
Coaches
Ekapon "Ek" Jantawong*: assistant coach

Nopparat Kanthawong: founder and head coach

Players
Chanin "Titan" Vibulrungruang*, eleven years old

Mongkol "Mark" Boonpiam*, twelve years old

Panumas "Mick" Sangdee*, thirteen years old

Duganpet "Dom" Promtep*, thirteen years old

Sompong "Pong" Jaiwong*, thirteen years old

Adul "Dul" Sam-on*, fourteen years old

Nattawut "Tern" Takamsong*, fourteen years old

Ekarat "Bew" Wongsukchan*, fourteen years old

Prajak "Note" Sutham*, fourteen years old

Pipat "Nick" Pho*, fifteen years old

Pornchai "Tee" Kamluang*, sixteen years old

Peerapat "Night" Sompiangjai*, seventeen years old

Thaweechai Nameng, thirteen years old

Songpul Kanthawong, thirteen years old

Thai Navy SEALs
Baitei: SEAL member who stayed with the team in the cave

Lieutenant Commander Saman Gunan: retired SEAL

Captain Anan Surawan

Thai Army
Dr. Pak Loharnshoon: medic who stayed with the team in the cave

Government Officials
General Prayut Chan-o-cha: prime minister of Thailand

Narongsak Osottanakorn: governor of Chiang Rai Province

Maha Vajiralongkorn Bodindradebayavarangkun: king of Thailand

Assisting in the Rescue

Ruengrit Changkwanyuen: diver
Sri Tammachoke: farmer

OTHER COUNTRIES

Australian

Craig Challen: cave diver
Dr. Richard "Harry" Harris: anesthesiologist and cave diver

British

Dr. Martin Ellis: geographer
Rob Harper: cave explorer
Chris Jewell: cave diver
Jason Mallinson: cave diver
Richard "Rick" Stanton, MBE: cave diver
Vernon Unsworth: cave explorer
John Volanthen: cave diver

Chinese

Wang Ke: volunteer member of the Beijing Peaceland Foundation
Zhou Yahui: volunteer member of the Beijing Peaceland Foundation

International Divers

Ivan Karadzic: Dane living in Thailand
Fernando Raigal: Spaniard
Ben Reymenants: Belgian living in Thailand

International Businessman

Elon Musk

United States Military

Master Sergeant Derek Anderson
Staff Sergeant James Brisbin
Staff Sergeant Michael Galindo
Major Charles Hodges: leader of US team at the cave
Captain Jessica Tait: chief public affairs officer for US effort

Prologue: Snatch and Grab
Thursday, June 28, 2018

CAVE DIVERS KNOW NOT TO PANIC; NOT TO LET THOUGHTS OF drowning linger and distract them. Make the best decision in this moment, this second, save your breath, stay alive. Face the next crisis when it comes.

Richard "Rick" Stanton and John Volanthen are two of the best cave divers in the world. They had flown overnight from England to Thailand to look for twelve Thai youth soccer players and their assistant coach, who, if alive, were somewhere deep in the pitch-dark, flooded caverns of the Tham Luang cave system. But now that the divers were in the cave, they realized that the best move was to give up the search.

The cave system was filled with so much rushing, muddy water that divers could not see even a foot in front of themselves. Even Stanton and Volanthen could not make any headway against the current. The boys were sealed in a watery trap. The divers finally managed to navigate far enough into the cavern to reach a large chamber where they found four terrified men.

Desperate to reduce the water level in the caves, authorities had managed to bring in water pumps operated by skilled workers and linked to long hoses that led out of the cavern. But the water had risen so quickly that four of the pump workers were trapped. The frightened men couldn't stay, couldn't make it through the tight tunnels that were flooded floor to ceiling, didn't know how to dive through the cold, muddy waters.

Stanton understood how to save a man who was in extreme danger but could not move: grasp him and pull him to safety. Back in England, he'd trained as a firefighter. Now, as the water in the chamber rose, he and Volanthen had to act, fast.

They'd have to grab the workmen, dive them back through to the cave entrance, and tell the Thai authorities to suspend the search for the boys: the rushing waters beyond the chamber were too dangerous to cross.

Cave diving is a new form of exploration that requires care, training, and specialized equipment, and Stanton and Volanthen are decorated, world-record-holding divers. That means they know when to quit, when the risk is just too high. For the moment, the hunt for the boys must end. Once they got the workmen out, going back into the cave would be suicide for the divers. Later on someone could go back to look for the boys—or their bodies.

1

Wild Boars

DR. ANDREW ALAN JOHNSON, AN AMERICAN ANTHROPOLOGIST who lived in northern Thailand for many years, has described the area near the Tham Luang cave system as a beautiful mountain valley with sharp-sided cliffs, the hills covered with green, dense jungle. And then comes the cave system, which is "enthralling. Its entrance is broad, like a cathedral door, and during the rainy season the humidity pours out of it like steam. It looks like the gateway to another world. In some senses, it is." Filled with inviting chambers, challenging tight corners, and branching paths, the caves are a popular destination for adventurous explorers, like the members of the Moo Pa youth soccer team.

The Moo Pa, or Wild Boars, were members of a soccer club whose players ranged in age from eleven to nineteen. Twelve players and their fit, outgoing, and good-humored assistant teacher-coach,

The entrance of the Tham Luang cave as seen from the inside, in the dry season.

twenty-five-year-old Ek (Ekapon Jantawong), had decided to cap off a day of practice by scrambling through the linked giant caverns and twisting, tight, and craggy passageways of the 6.4-mile-(10.3-kilometer)-long cave system.

Nopparat Kanthawong, the team's creator and head coach, started the group in 2015 as a free activity to give young people, especially those facing difficult lives, a chance to enjoy themselves and to improve their skills. When about seventy players across a wide range of ages joined up, Coach Kanthawong divided the players into four age groups, though the best players could "play up" into the next squad. The players in the cave cut across the age groups.

The Wild Boars practiced hard, sent some graduates on to

major Thai soccer teams, and fared surprisingly well in regional tournaments—earning second place in one recent contest and taking home the championship in another. But their bonds went beyond sports. Ek created a system where an athlete's playtime was linked to how he was doing in school. Excitement about sports led to better study habits, and better grades guaranteed more chances to excel at sports. The sports-school link was only part of what the team offered.

Out of the seventy Wild Boars, at least twenty—including three lost in the cave and Ek himself—were not Thai; their place in the country was fragile. As Coach Kanthawong explained, "All of the kids who join the team, they all wish that they would be professional soccer players. But they would not be able to do so if they don't have nationalities." Ek and the other "stateless" players were among the 400,000 to possibly as many as three million people in Thailand who are similar to what are called "undocumented" immigrants in the United States, with an added level of peril. They are not Thai, but if they are missing any birth information from their home country, they are also no longer citizens of the lands in which they were born.

Stateless people can live in Thailand but do not have the legal papers that would allow them to study, travel, and work throughout the country, eventually get married, or leave Thailand and return. As the coach said, they have no nationality at all. The team is a kind of home—a place to be together, bond, share, and learn away from the impossible pressure of being a person without a country.

As Ek tells it, they had been thinking about exploring the caves for a while, ever since they'd gone on a team-building bike trip together. "Hey," he remembered someone saying, "let's go to Tham

Luang on the next trip." Ek and three of the players had already visited the cave several times, but that only made the others more eager to get their chance.

The players who planned to visit the cave included **Titan** (Chanin Vibulrungruang), who was eleven and the youngest member of the team. "Titan" is a Thai pronunciation of the English word. Many Thai people are given nicknames at birth, which may often be Thai pronunciations of English words, and use those nicknames all the time except on the most formal, official occasions where they use their given first names. Though Titan was born in Thailand, his grandmother was not. He was able to visit relatives on both sides of the Thai border whenever he liked, but when she visits him, she, too, is stateless. Usually a lively, happy person with a high-pitched voice, Titan had been playing soccer for five years and liked to be a forward or a striker.

Mark (Mongkol Boonpiam) was twelve, in seventh grade, and known for rooting for Real Madrid and paying close attention to games in the Spanish elite La Liga. Like Ek, Adul, and Tee, Mark was born in Burma (also known as Myanmar) and was stateless in Thailand. ("Burma" was renamed Myanmar by its government when it was run by its military. Some who are critical of the former military rulers continue to use the older name.) Mark was as intent on his studies as on his game.

At thirteen, **Mick** (Panumas Sangdee), a seventh grader, was one of the younger players, but he was agile and big for his age and enjoyed being a midfielder. **Dom** (Duganpet Promtep) was also thirteen and in seventh grade. He was known for inspiring other players, had been named captain of the team, and had been scouted by adult Thai teams. His girlfriend, thirteen-year-old Nutchanan Ramkeaw, said he was actually scared of the dark but for that very reason liked the challenge of entering caves in order to be brave and to overcome his fears.

Later, as the story of the lost team spread over Thai media, pictures of Dom and Mark attracted special attention. Social networks buzzed with comments on how handsome they were.

Pong (Sompong Jaiwong) was thirteen, in seventh grade, played left wing, and was an avid sports fan—whether playing soccer or watching the World Cup (which was taking place just as the team entered the cave). He was rooting for England.

Fourteen-year-old Adul Sam-on—whose name was sometimes shortened to Dul—was in eighth grade, played left defender, and was known for his skill with languages, as he spoke Thai, Burmese, Chinese, Wa, and English—in Chinese class he sometimes used the name Chen Ning. Born in Burma, Adul is ethnically Wa and was stateless within Thailand. Historically the Wa lived high on hills across China and Burma. Fiercely independent, they have an area within Burma they consider their own state, and control their own army. This has led to a series of clashes, and temporary peace treaties, with the Burmese government. Unlike the overwhelming majority of Thai people, the Wa are not Buddhist and have been visited by both Buddhist and Christian missionaries. Adul, for example, was Christian.

Tern (Nattawut Takamsong) was fourteen, in eighth grade, and was relatively new to the team. He was the kind of person who took pride in being able to take care of himself. At fourteen, **Bew** (Ekarat Wongsukchan) was in eighth grade, and was the team's main goalie. **Note** (Prajak Sutham) was also fourteen and in eighth grade. He rooted for a local team, Chiang Rai United, and played both goalie and midfielder. Fifteen-year-old **Nick** (Pipat Pho) was a close friend of Bew's and in ninth grade. He was not actually on the team yet but came to the practice and followed on to the cave. **Tee** (Pornchai Kamluang) was sixteen, in tenth grade, a defender, and had discussed the trip with his girlfriend before the team went into the cave. Tee was ethnically Tai Yai. Born in Burma, he too was stateless in Thailand.

Finally, **Night** (Peerapat Sompiangjai), who turned seventeen the day the team entered the cave, was in ninth grade and was a right winger. (Some Thai people who use the nickname "Night" prefer to see it as "Knight"—which of course is possible, since the English words sound the same.)

Saturday, June 23

The team planned out the day carefully. First, starting at ten in the morning, they played a warm-up game about two miles (3.2 kilometers) from the caves. After they finished the match, they biked over to the caves, "since everyone was curious." The caves, which are an international as well as local attraction in the dry season, beckoned, but the team members were all watching the clock. One player needed to be back by five o'clock to meet his tutor. Night's parents had planned a birthday party for him, complete with SpongeBob cakes. The whole team had been invited to come, and no one wanted to disappoint his parents by being late. Once they reached the cave, they would have about four hours to explore its inviting caverns.

Around noon the team biked over to Tham Luang with their backpacks and had lunch and snacks. The interlinked corridors of the cave system are dry—sometimes. The sequence of chambers and narrow passages weaves its way inside limestone hills that were once the bottom of an ancient seabed. Created through the endless accumulation, combination, and crushing of seashells, limestone resembles hardened sponges.

The full name of the cave system is Tham Luang Nang Non— "the Royal Cave of the Reclining Woman," and there is a story behind the name. The cave is located in the far northern corner of Thailand. This wedge of the country is so close to Burma and Laos that it is called the Golden Triangle. The term is not meant as a compliment—the loose borders were exploited for many years by drug smugglers bringing first opium and later methamphetamine from creators to markets. The Thai government helped to shut down the opium traffic, but the drug smuggling is so well known in the area that there is a museum called the Hall of Opium that seeks to entice curious tourists. And the easy pathways from one nation to another are one reason why there are many stateless people in the area. A family may bring a child across the border to Thailand to give him or her a better start in life—even though the child will face the challenge of not having Thai residency papers. The overlapping histories of peoples in the region can also be seen in the story of the cave.

According to the legend, many years ago a princess from Burma fell in love with a man who was not royal, and she became pregnant. Her parents were furious, and she fled from them into the cave. When her father's soldiers followed her, she took her own life. Her body is said to have formed the mountains, and the cave is the passage in—haunted by wounded, angry spirits. The spirits look like a cross between ogres and giants. They are frightening but also in pain, and capable of being healed. A modern shrine to the spirit of the princess stands at the cave mouth. As Dr. Johnson explains, a common view in Thailand is that you don't need to believe in spirits, but you also don't want to offend them.

There is good reason to treat the caves with respect. Interlaced with countless crevices and tiny tunnels, the limestone walls of the cave are extremely porous. For four months of the year, storm systems begin gathering moisture over the Indian Ocean and sweep across Thailand. These monsoons send black clouds scudding across the sky and pour down sheets of driving rain. The falling water cascades through the rocks, creating flash floods that inundate the cave. Caverns instantly become lakes, tight passageways fill floor to ceiling with water, and the slope of the ground creates a current flowing from deep in the cave system out toward its mouth. That enticing gateway now gushes water—looking, the Belgian diver Ben Reymenants has said, like white water churning on the Colorado River. A sign warns no one to enter during the rainy season from July to November. But since it was still June and the previous year the rains did not begin until mid-July, the team thought they were safe.

A guide to the caves describes them as being at the bottom of a "magnificent" semicircle of cliffs filled with "lush evergreen forest."

The wide opening Dr. Johnson described invites explorers to enter, and for about a half mile (one kilometer) there is an easy walk, part of which is paved with cement. From there visitors navigate through boulders until the passage narrows down to a space some six and a half feet (two meters) wide and about ten feet (three meters) high. Past the opening chamber, the caverns let in no light and there are no pathways. Explorers need to wedge themselves between jagged rocks, finding pathways up, down, into and out of whatever space they can manage to see. Those who make it through soon reach even tighter tunnels in which they need to crawl to reach the next high, open chamber. From the easy entry to the challenging crevices, the caves drew Ek and the boys ever farther into their depths.

Guided by their flashlights, the team navigated through the caves for about three hours until they reached a spot they called the Labyrinthine/Groundwater City. The chamber was filled with water and they had to decide: keep going or turn back. Most could swim well—and even those who were beginners were willing to try. They'd all be cold and wet for a bit, but the depths of the cave were calling. After all, in dry season, even school groups came to the caves and managed to make their way through them.

Tee, one of the older members of the team, jumped into the water to test how deep it was and said it was fine all the way across. Ek followed and agreed, but it was getting late. They had better turn around, Tee warned, and they began walking back. Marching into a wide-mouthed dry cave is one thing. Scrambling against time in a dark cave filling with water is another.

Thaweechai Nameng, who had explored the cave with his friends but whose parents made him come home after the game, explained that "when you're in the cave, you don't hear the rain." When the rain really hit "and the water started flowing," they must have been "too far inside."

The path ahead split into two branches and they were not sure where to go to get back. Bew noticed water rising. "Are we lost?" someone asked. Some of the boys were starting to get scared—scared that they might be lost, trapped in the cave. Scared that they would arrive home late and their parents would be angry—they had all made sure not to tell the adults that they had planned to explore the cave after the game.

Ek, who is genial and gracious, reassured the team that "there's one way back—the way we came from." He decided to go ahead into the flow of water with three of the boys: Tee, Night, and Adul. The water was so high now that he would have to dive to see if they could swim to the next chamber. How could the other three know where he was? Ek had a rope and left one end with the group waiting for him. If he yanked twice, that would mean he was in trouble and they must pull him back. If he sent no signal, he had found a passage and they should follow.

Ek plunged into the water, but he soon began "running out of breath." One tug, two. Night pulled him out. They could not dive across the water and needed to find another escape route. One possibility was to dig out a channel to redirect the water that was blocking them. That way they could see the path back. Everyone grabbed stones and started chipping at the rocks. It was nearing five p.m.—their parents would be angry, would be worried, and the cave was very dark. Scraping the limestone, they worked to divert the water, but after what felt like an hour, they realized they were getting nowhere. The water was rising. Tee wondered if they should stop trying to get out and instead look for a safe place to rest. Ek, calm as ever, agreed with Tee that the rising water might be a tide, which would ebb again if they waited it out. Instead of fighting the moment, they needed to find a place to regroup, rest, and wait. Retreating back into the cave, they found sand mounds that would keep them dry, and water dripping from the walls that was clean enough to drink.

Ek and the team were lost in a pitch-black cave with no way to reach the outside world, no food, and rising water. But for the moment, they were safe.

Saturday Night, June 23
OUTSIDE THE CAVE

Five o'clock came and went. None of the boys or the coach returned—for lessons, for the party—and their parents began to worry. Mick's girlfriend kept texting him, desperately trying to find out where they were. One Wild Boar, thirteen-year-old Songpul Kanthawong, had come home after the practice. He didn't have a bike so he couldn't join his friends in the adventure. By nine that night his uncle, the team's head coach, called. "Do you know where Ek is?" he asked. "They went to the cave," Songpul answered.

Coach Kanthawong rushed to the cave, as did Sungwat Kummongkol, a local rescue worker, and found the team's bikes carefully parked with cleats neatly lined up beside each one. The boys had planned their trip and had entered the cave, but where were they? How long could they last? And now the torrential rains were pouring down and the cave was filling up with even more water.

Kummongkol contacted other rescuers who had dive equipment, but they could not squeeze their gas canisters into the tight caverns.

"Ek! Ek! Ek!" Coach Kanthawong screamed into the cave. His "body went completely cold." The boys and Ek were gone. Families, local police, friends rushed to the cave. Calling for their lost sons, their voices echoed and then faded into silence.

2

SEALs and Cave Divers
Sunday, June 24

Midnight

AT FIRST, NO ONE OUTSIDE OF THOSE CLOSE TO THE TEAM KNEW they were missing. By midnight, Narongsak Osottanakorn, the governor of Chiang Rai Province, learned of the missing team and came to the cave an hour later. Known as highly skilled, honest, and devoted to protecting the environment in his province, Osottanakorn was the kind of leader who would drop everything to help out in what otherwise might have seemed like a local mishap. Constant rain was making the cave entrance impassible; the local divers realized they could not be of use and left.

By morning more and more concerned people were coming to help, but as one person told a reporter from the BBC, "no one really had any idea what to do." Some brought pumps and pipes, whatever they had at hand, to try to pull water out of the cave. But that was like trying to divert a river with a garden hose. Policemen managed to get far enough into the cave to find handprints left by the boys—a sign they had retreated farther into the cave system. To enter those depths, the police would need expert help. Someone contacted Vernon Unsworth, an Englishman who lived in Thailand and had spent a lot of time exploring these caves—in the dry season.

The cave system split in a kind of T, with one arm leading up in what maps call the Monk Series. Unsworth said no one would go that way, as the passage quickly narrowed to a crawl. Anyone retreating from the water would have taken the other arm toward a sandy bank called Pattaya Beach. But the space where the arms met in a T-junction was totally flooded. Only expert divers could possibly cross it. Governor Osottanakorn contacted the Royal Thai Navy and requested that they send their SEALs. If anyone could manage the cave, which is considered one of the five most dangerous in the world when it is flooded, it would be the SEALs.

SEALs

During World War II, the US Navy began creating units of "frogmen"—sailors trained to be so adept underwater they could scout out enemy coastal positions or destroy enemy seaside arma- ments. As the D-Day landing began at Omaha Beach in Normandy, France, navy divers went ahead to blow up the deadly barriers the Germans had placed in the water, and lost one out of every two men to enemy fire. Frogmen, nicknamed "naked warriors," were equally brave in preparing the way for the island-by-island combat in the Pacific. In the early 1960s, when the first Americans were sent into orbit around the earth, their Mercury capsules were designed to splash down in the open ocean. Navy divers helped to recover the astronauts bobbing in the water. Slowly, over the 1950s and early 1960s, these hardy, amphibious naval units evolved into Sea, Air, and Land (SEAL) special forces teams. As their name suggests, special forces were not limited to water. SEALs were trained to do whatever was needed, wherever, and under all conditions.

Some of the secret missions SEAL units were tasked with carrying out have drawn criticism from observers and even questions from the fighters. One Cold War program required SEALs to carry backpack nuclear bombs—though none were ever used; another, during the war in Vietnam, trained "men with green faces" (camouflage face paint for the dense jungles) to carry out targeted assassinations. Today SEALs are known for the rigorous physical and psychological training they go through, for accomplishing difficult missions—such as capturing and killing Osama Bin Laden, the architect of the 9/11 terrorist attacks—and for their ability to function under cover in many environments.

Since 1952 Thailand has had its own SEAL unit, whose intense training closely matches that of its American ally. In both countries, due to the sensitive nature of their missions, the names of active-duty SEALs are not made public, and when they give interviews, their faces are covered. In Thailand, where the military intervened and took over the government in 2014, human rights and democracy advocates are quite critical of the armed forces. Yet if any Thai personnel could find the boys, it would be the SEALs.

And as more and more people in Thailand became aware of

the missing team, political and regional divisions faded away. As one Twitter user posted: "It makes me realize that this country still has hopes, and a big heart. People in the country dropped their biases and are helping each other. They all help pray for the Moo Pa team to survive. I hope you are safe, brothers." Thailand's king, Maha Vajiralongkorn Bodindradebayavarangkun, who spends a great deal of time in Munich, Germany, made it known that he was focused on the boys and the effort to rescue them. A local crisis was becoming a national obsession. The buzz in Thailand soon drew journalists from international publications. The cave story was becoming international hot news, with updates cycling across crawlers on the bottoms of screens.

Like the original frogmen, Thai SEALs are skilled at functioning in water, whether that means training bare-chested in pools filled with chunks of ice or mastering the scuba outfit that allows people to swim underwater. The basic scuba equipment is a tank containing compressed air, a mouthpiece, and a valve to regulate the flow of gas to the swimmer. Most divers worldwide use scuba gear to swim in open water. Then there are the cave divers. While the SEALs would bring courage, discipline, and gas tanks to the search, they were not among the very small group of people worldwide who are expert at swimming through flooded caves.

The Danish cave diver Ivan Karadzic lives in Thailand. He got the message that some boys were lost in northern Thailand. But word was it was a few boys and they were probably somewhere near the entrance. Ivan went off for his own three-hour exploration of a different cave. When he came out of the water, the full story was all over the media. He rushed to offer his services. Ivan sees "cave diving" as a highly specialized form of diving: "a niche within a niche."

"Scuba diving is a sport, a hobby," Karadzic explains, "something many people do for fun." There are hazards diving in the open ocean or a large lake, but in general those dangers can be predicted and prevented. Cave diving is something else entirely. Rick Stanton has described cave diving as more uncertain and unknown than even exploring the moon. "With cave diving," he told an interviewer in 2007, "you don't know whether to go up, down, left or right."

Karadzic agrees: "Cave diving means exploring submerged caves, entering areas that have been undisturbed for hundreds of thousands or even millions of years. You must master basic diving—train in a lake or open water. You must have above-average diving skill and have learned to use the equipment carefully and precisely. You may be in situations that are incredibly uncomfortable: narrow spaces; long periods of low or no visibility. In exchange, you have out-of-this-world experiences, you are in another world, weightless, in zero gravity, and this creates an almost mystical feeling. You are explorers, but you must have the training, the certification, to dive safely."

As SEALs gathered at the cave, one after another, Karadzic and other trained cave divers volunteered to join them. The good news was that more and more people were coming to the cave. That was also the bad news. William Stone, an expert American cave diver and cave rescuer, has said that the best cave rescues are the ones

This image, taken in Peña Colorada cave in Mexico gives a hint of how cave divers need to bring everything with them, even the air they breathe.

you never hear about. Only the key rescuers are allowed on the site, and they do their work unseen, undisturbed. Everyone else—family, media, volunteers, people not trained for this special mission—are kept away. With lives at stake, only people who have specific, professional skills and experience at making difficult decisions should be involved. No one would want random spectators and anxious family members in a hospital operating room—just trained nurses and doctors. The scene at the Tham Luang cave was the absolute opposite.

One part of the space in front of the cave mouth was given to the families, as well as Buddhist priests there to offer prayers, assistance, and comfort. Teachers from the schools the Wild Boars attended arrived. "We wanted to be the first to welcome the boys when they came out," an administrator named Ampin Saenta told a reporter. Indeed, media from the entire world were now flocking to the site, as many as fifteen to sixteen hundred print, video, radio, and TV reporters along with their sound and camera crews. To feed this growing instant city, in which languages from across the globe were being spoken, a group of volunteers set up kitchens to cook, a second marshaled tubs filled with hot water and electric washer-dryers to clean everyone's clothing, and a third put out chairs so people could sit and have their hair trimmed.

Like everyone in Thailand, Narinthorn Na Bangchang, a Thai singer and actress, heard about the team lost in the cave. Her assistant mentioned that his brother, Ruengrit Changkwanyuen, was a cave diver who could help train the SEALS in how to apply their open-water skills to the flooded cave and had the equipment they would need. The singer and the instructor dashed to the cave to meet the SEALs.

This outburst of volunteering—all the food and services was donated, given away for free—is a testament to the generosity and goodwill of the Thai people. And there was more. As the rains continued to fill the caves, a new line of attack was suggested: Would it be possible to squeeze down through the limestone hills and bring the boys up and out that way? Eight Muslim men from Trang Province in southern Thailand, who hunt for specific birds' nests to be gathered, sold, and used in recipes, learned about the rescue efforts. Since they are expert rock climbers with sharp eyes, they

Ruengrit Changkwanyuen, second from the left, is a General Motors manager who brought his cave-diving expertise to the cave. On the far right is the Belgian diver Ben Reymenants.

offered to come and comb the hills for gaps that could be expanded. Soldiers tried rappelling down ropes into crevices. A Muslim woman named Sophia Thaianant realized that, like the birds' nest hunters, some of the people helping out in the rescue were Muslim and could only eat food prepared according to Muslim dietary laws. She and her friends began making one hundred, then two hundred, meals a day for free, while others turned out the up to five thousand meal packs needed to feed the growing crowds. Day by day the hills and the cave filled with ever more people using their skills, trying to help.

But whether it was SEALs trained to dive in open water, cave

Three of the eight birds' nest collectors who traveled from southern Thailand to help look for alternate entrances to the cave in which the team was trapped.

divers arriving on their own without direction, the hum of searching and climbing on the hills, or the swirl of well-wishers, reporters, religious figures, and family at the cave entrance, it was not clear whether all this effort could bring anyone closer to finding the boys.

Or whether it might be making the rescue impossible.

3

The Cave System
Monday and Tuesday, June 25-26

RAINS RUSHED DOWN, BLANKETING THE HILLS AND FILLING THE interlocking chambers of the cave system with water. Hollowed out of the limestone, the caves were edged in sharp rocks, with stalactites hanging down like craggy inverted pyramids and stalagmites thrusting up like miniature mountains. Where the passageways narrowed to tight tunnels, water completely filled the space, floor to ceiling. Divers were no longer swimmers gliding over the current; they were in total darkness and completely immersed—as if they were swimming through a filled, sealed tube—with unpredictable hazards all around them. Each one needed to bring his own supply of air, light, and rope.

The first step in exploring a new cave is what divers call "laying line." The Spanish diver Fernando Raigal works in many places but is based in Thailand. He came to help out. He explained how this works: "As you enter the cave, you carry a coil of rope and attach one end at the start. You secure it and carefully spool it out as you go bit by bit. The rope line is both a way out if you need it and a guide for the next diver. You are creating the path as you are using it."

In order to find the team, rescuers would need to work their way through the caves, laying line as they went. Swimming through flooded caves is an exercise in math and physics. The diver must calculate how many tanks to carry, what mix of gases is in each tank (depending on the depth of the dive, the proportion of oxygen, nitrogen, and even helium varies), and then, as the Belgian diver Ben Reymenants explained, you split that total into thirds. One-third of the gas is to get you to your goal, one-third to bring you back, and one-third in case of emergency. In a complicated and flooded cave system, even tanks and math would not be enough. It would be certain suicide to send in one diver with a few tanks. Where possible—if any caverns held dry spots—the SEALs would need to stow air canisters and food. Each cache would be a landing and resupply point that would allow divers to press ahead and search the next set of caverns.

Monday, 2:45 a.m.

Twenty Thai SEALs, led by Captain Anan Surawan, whose thin, bespectacled face betrayed a sense of the weight of responsibility he carried, arrived at the scene. The cave was relatively dry for much of the way to the T-junction so the SEALs could actually walk in and reach the large cavern that would come to be called Chamber Three. An hour's walk from there they reached the T-junction, which was now under 6 feet (1.8 meters) of water. Guided by the British cave

Four of the Thai Navy SEALs who were willing to risk everything to help with the rescue, even though their dive training was in open water and not in the more treacherous caves. Because of the sensitive nature of their missions, active duty SEALs cover their faces and do not release their names.

explorer Vernon Unsworth's instructions, the SEALs crossed it and reached about 125 yards (115 meters) into the cave in the direction of Pattaya Beach, leaving behind a distinctive piece of webbing as a marker of their progress.

"We went in a few kilometers and were able to enter a second chamber behind the entrance," a Thai SEAL told a reporter for the British newspaper the *Guardian*. "In that chamber, there was an area where I saw shoes and bags left behind on the ground. We believe the students have gone further in." At least now everyone knew that

Unsworth was right: the team had headed toward Pattaya Beach, even if they were no longer there. Unsworth added, "If they're in the right place, they can survive for five or six days. But the water now, the floodwater, is getting higher and higher, so there will be a point in time where even this cave here, the entrance will close."

To reach Pattaya Beach, divers would need to enter the cave and again cross the T-junction where the two main branches of the cave system split. For the moment, that was impossible. At the junction, a rapid current of murky, muddy water was filling the cavern to the ceiling. Even with lights, divers could not see in front of themselves and would run out of air before making any real progress. Anupong Paochinda, a high Thai official, told reporters that "Divers are in dark areas that are not flat and there's mud and rocks everywhere. Therefore, for the SEAL team that's there, when they dive, sometimes one tank can only go as far as thirty meters [ninety-eight feet] and they have to turn back."

The driving rain created three daunting, interconnected challenges:

1. There was no way to stop rain from falling and flooding the caves. But could water be pumped out to dry the caverns? More and larger pumps began to arrive from throughout Thailand to battle the rainfall and attempt to lower the water levels in the caves.

2. The more water, the more difficult and dangerous it would be to try to dive through the caves. Thai SEALs were not

trained for this kind of mission. Could anyone in the world help them?

3. If the water could not be held back or dived through, was there any other way into the cave?

Outside the cave, more volunteers and gifts arrived: the king's sister sent fifteen thousand raincoats. Far off in Zimbabwe, Wang Ke and other members of the Beijing Peaceland Foundation—a group of Chinese volunteers who help out in rescues when they learn of disasters—were working to protect endangered animals from poachers. Hearing about the lost boys, Wang Ke wondered

Beyond the cave entrance, all light had to be brought in, or came from headlamps worn by workers.

if they could be of use but assumed that by the time they got there, the boys would be safe. As reports reached him of the continuing drama and the flood of volunteers, he changed plans. He would fly back to China, then join other members of the foundation at the cave. Indeed, cave divers from Ireland to Singapore, Argentina to Canada, were buying tickets, getting on planes, rushing to the caves. The swell of people from all over, though, also presented opportunities for thieves, who mingled with the crowds and broke into cars. People claiming spiritual powers arrived to cast spells and commune with spirits. Even as conditions grew ever worse, and the chances of reaching the boys seemed more remote, the chaotic throng at the cave mouth grew and grew.

Tuesday

Heavy rains were making conditions extremely difficult. Where the first SEALs had been able to walk deep into the caverns, now the water was so high that the T-junction was entirely filled and Chamber Three was flooding. Soon there would be so little air that even the divers would be in danger. Anyone who wanted to look for the boys would need to be able to swim from Chamber Three to the T-junction and beyond. The SEALs had never worked underwater in caves. They needed help.

Unsworth knew of the very best cave divers and cave rescuers in the world—Rick Stanton and John Volanthen. He sent a note with their names and that of Rob Harper from Britain—who had explored the cave system with Unsworth and the geographer Martin Ellis—urging Thai authorities to reach out to them at once. The

As the water filled the cave, it even began flowing out of the entrance. Since no one could stop the rain, workers did everything possible to set up pumps and pipelines to drain the water.

Thai government immediately agreed. By Tuesday night, Stanton, Volanthen, and Harper were on their way to Thailand. The government also recognized that all this effort would fail unless it was organized and given structure. They contacted the US military and requested that a team of experts come to map a strategy and parcel out tasks.

The rain kept falling, and the water in the caves kept rising. As volunteers tried to load pumps into the caverns, half the equipment banged, crashed, fell, and was so damaged it was useless. The remaining pumps could not keep pace. The SEALs could not recross the T-junction, and more and more people were coming to the caves. Somewhere between crisis, chaos, and hope, the desperate search for the boys continued.

Deep in the Cave

Assistant Coach Ek and the twelve young men had no idea what was going on all around them. They could not hear the hundreds of soldiers or the team of bird's-nest collectors spread across the hills above, the pumps going twenty-four hours a day at the cave mouth, the calls and prayers of their parents, the splash of the SEALs diving against the force of the current, trying to enter the cave. They were perched on a small sandy bank, meditating.

Ek felt responsible for putting the team in danger; he was going to do anything possible to help them survive. Fortunately, he had experience facing adversity and managing extremely challenging circumstances. He was born in Burma, a member of the Shan people. The Shan probably originated in China and spread across what are now China, Burma, and the Golden Triangle area of Thailand. For centuries, very much like farmers in medieval Europe, the Shan had defined themselves through loyalty to local princes, who in turn paid tribute to distant kings. In the nineteenth and twentieth centuries, when mapmakers far away drew firm national borders, the Shan did not quite fit. Within Burma, the Shan controlled an area of their own but battled the government for more self-control. And some Shan were now considered Thai. By the time Ek was ten, both of his parents and his brother had died. After two years of being a "sad and lonely" boy, Ek was taken by his relatives to a Buddhist monastery in Thailand to be raised. Not only was he orphaned, but living in Thailand, he was stateless. While he could get an education and receive limited government health care, he would not obtain the mandatory "residency card" that would allow him to travel throughout Thailand or to other countries. As part of his Buddhist training, though, he learned to meditate, a crucial survival skill he decided to share now with the boys.

As we each go through the day, our minds are filled with thoughts, feelings, needs—all of which seem extremely important. In "mindfulness" meditation, a person sits calmly with legs crossed and breathes slowly, focusing on the sensation of air coming in and going out. As the meditator's attention zeroes in on breath, it is possible to watch the content of the mind. The same thoughts, feelings, needs flicker across, but step by step, as breath comes in and out, the meditator notices each one. Instead of thinking, *This is what I am, this is what I want,* the meditator can begin to observe those yearnings from a distance. As Professor Johnson explains, you can "see your emotions, feel them, and let them go."

Western scientists have recently come to agree with the long-standing Buddhist belief that this sort of practice can be very beneficial. It can help to calm, relax, and center a person. Ek learned to meditate in the monastery and kept it up after he left. According to his aunt, Ek would spend as much as an hour each day practicing this kind of meditation, and now he shared the exercise with the team. Of course they were hungry, scared, worried about having not told their parents about the cave trip. Meditating helped each one keep fear away and be in the present. They could not control the future, but they could work to relax their minds. Meditation was a gift Ek could give them. At every moment they could see his cheerful face and feel his caring attention watching them, guiding them, holding them close and offering protection.

At first everyone felt strong, but by what must have been the second day, some of the boys began to weaken from hunger. Ek counseled them to remain still, to fill up on water licked from the overhanging stalactites, and to hold off using their flashlights to save the batteries. Titan, the youngest and thinnest, began feeling dizzy and focusing on the delicious food he missed. But he distracted himself by shifting his thoughts to plainer dishes: fried rice and chili paste. Under Ek's watchful eye, even hunger could be managed.

4

The Most Dangerous Sport
Wednesday and Thursday, June 27–28

WEDNESDAY, KADENA AIR BASE, OKINAWA, JAPAN. "THERE IS A soccer team stuck in a cave in Thailand, be ready, we are being notified that we might head out." Major Charles Hodges, a Citadel honors graduate with a Boy Scout's can-do attitude, was put on notice by his director of operations. Hodges is commander of the US Air Force's 320th Special Tactics Squadron, and they were needed right away. This is the kind of mission Hodges enjoys—a challenge that would call on their training in organizing rescues under difficult circumstances, with the added incentive of the chance to help out, to be of service, to young people in danger.

Hodges would have to pull together a team of no more than thirty-four soldiers from his group and the pararescue specialists from the 31st Rescue Squadron—as he'd have exactly thirty-five seats available on the packed C-130 plane that would ferry them to

Thailand. One of those slots was reserved for a native Thai speaker on his team. Having one Thai speaker was a start, though Hodges knew that language was the least of their concerns. For decades, US military efforts have been conducted as part of multinational teams, and there are training sessions for officers in how to work well with peers from different backgrounds. He knew that differences of culture and outlook might be harder to bridge than matters of language. The Thai government had invited the United States to come help, and the Thais were, as they should be, in charge. But Hodges and his team were there to use their own professional judgment. What would happen if Thai officials and US officers had different visions of the mission?

Captain Jessica Tait, the well-spoken chief public affairs officer for the 353rd Special Operations Group, and Master Sergeant Derek Anderson, who has the I-can-handle-anything demeanor of a catcher on a baseball team, hustled through the morning, got their gear together, and clambered into the plane.

The C-130 carrying the squad taxied along the runway, then suddenly came to a stop. While its engines roared, the plane remained motionless, with thirty-four soldiers in their seats wondering what was happening. Finally a commercial airline on its scheduled route touched down. Its doors opened, steps unfurled, and a man wearing casual shorts and a T-shirt rushed down and across the tarmac. Staff Sergeant James Brisbin had been on vacation with his family in the beautiful temple city of Kyoto but had bought a ticket to return to base on the twenty-seventh. Brisbin was a member of the 31st Rescue Squadron and had been a cave diver before joining the military. The last seat on the C-130 was reserved for him. Now complete, the American crew took off for Thailand, knowing very little about what was ahead of them. They would arrive at one in the morning the next day, Thai time, with one interpreter, one cave diver, a team experienced in rescues, an unknown mission—and the entire world watching.

Across the globe in Zimbabwe, Wang Ke was contacting the Chinese embassy in Thailand, offering his services and sending a request to members of his Peaceland Foundation, looking for volunteers with "professional cave exploration and diving skills."

By six in the evening, the British divers reached Bangkok, where they were bundled into a minibus and sped to the cave. Rick Stanton is one of those people whose features suggest the most intense focus. John Volanthen, his cave-diving partner, works as an IT specialist, and it is not hard to picture him as the scoutmaster he is, combining a hearty eagerness with a careful, skeptical gaze. Stanton and Volanthen came to Thailand with Rob Harper, who would serve as coordinator of the British team. Stanton and Volanthen, along with Chris Jewell and Jason Mallinson, were perhaps the most skilled, fearless cave divers in the world. If anyone could find a way past the rushing current, across the T-junction, through the extremely narrow "pinch points" to wherever the boys might be, it would be this team. After all, Stanton, Volanthen, and Mallinson, along with Dutch diver Rene Houben, had set a world record in 2010 when they spent fifty hours penetrating 5.5 miles (8.8 kilometers) through the Pozo Azul cave system in Spain.

Martyn Farr, himself a cave diver and author of *The Darkness*

Beckons, one of the best books on the subject, met the divers as they began the assault on Pozo Azul. As he noted in his diary, "They are like icebergs: above water you see just a minute part; below the surface there is unfathomable strength and indefatigable resolve." To Farr, the Pozo Azul dive was as dangerous, and significant, as the first recorded climb of Mount Everest or trip to the North Pole. One challenge in 2010 was that both Stanton and Mallinson were eager to take on the greatest risks. In the end it was Mallinson who reached the farthest point. He attributed his success to "a strong survival instinct, no panic, along with bail-out options which were barely adequate."

Calmness, courage, planning: the cave-diving credo.

Both Stanton and Volanthen had been introduced to cave diving as teenagers. Volanthen had explored dry caves as a Boy Scout and found them all the more enticing with the added challenge of water. Stanton first heard about cave diving from a Scout and thought, *I'd love to do something like that.* A year or so later, when he was eighteen, his mother asked him to come see a show on TV. It "was about two divers linking up what was then the longest cave dive in the world. After watching it, I just knew that cave diving was for me." Though he went on to college and enjoyed a career as a firefighter, from the moment he saw the show, he had found his calling. As Stanton says, in cave diving he has found a passion that has "guided his life" from then to now. "If you are lucky," he explains, "you find something that identifies you." For him that is cave diving, which he does not see as a sport or hobby. It is a physical and mental activity that involves thinking and planning, logistics, challenges to overcome, exploration, people you meet—friends you create for life.

The passion for cave diving, with all its dangers, does not mean Stanton, Volanthen, and Mallinson are the kind of adventure addicts who take risks for the rush of speeding up the pulse. The very fact that you are entering an unknown and hostile environment in which you need to carry with you even the air you are to breathe, in which visibility may be minimal and there is a danger of sharp objects and entrapping dead ends at every turn, means you must be very well prepared and clear-thinking. Volanthen has said that "diving to great depths involves complete commitment to an increasingly hazardous situation." Hazardous indeed: cave diving has been called the world's most dangerous sport. For example, between 1960 and 1980, 194 cave divers were killed in Florida alone. A survey of the entire United States shows how dangerous the sport still is, but how it has improved since then. Between 1985 and 2015, 161 divers across the fifty states were killed in caves. The difference is due to the strict guidelines and proper training procedures that have been developed. But the death rate shows how careful you must be. "You're in an environment that doesn't suffer fools gladly," Volanthen has said. What he and Stanton strive for in a dive is clarity and precision, not excitement. "Panic and adrenaline are great in certain situations," he explains, "but not in cave diving."

When Stanton and Volanthen reached the Tham Luang cave, they found complete chaos. The entrance was shoulder to shoulder with reporters taping segments, film crews wrestling their equipment from spot to spot, rescuers, and volunteers. There was no one to greet and guide them, though they did find Unsworth, who warned that Chamber Three was overflowing, flooding the passage out. Cameras and microphones followed the divers everywhere, even as they had to push their way through the scrum to enter the cave, commandeering the tanks and ropes they needed as they went. Someone warned them not to try to go farther into the cave, but a Thai SEAL said the choice was theirs. One challenge would be the cave, another would be the crowd.

The C-130 landed on time at one in the morning on the twenty-eighth. Major Hodges sent most off to rest, but he and his fellow team leaders headed straight to the cave entrance for a first meeting with the Thai SEALs. Captain Tait did not have a headlamp, so she could not see in front of herself; she could only try to stay close enough to those who did. Then she thought of the soccer team, deep in the enveloping darkness: she could not "even imagine" what they might be experiencing. Major Hodges surveyed the site and made a few mental notes. High on the cave walls he saw mud lines—an indication of just how far up water flows could reach. And then, scattered through the cave floor, he saw "sumps." A sump is a hollow or pathway beneath the rock—which can fill with water and be any length and depth, from a short muddy crawl to a long, dangerous dive. One reason why British divers happen to be so adept in caves is that sumps are a frequent feature in the caves of their homeland. As they train in their beloved sport, they gain practice in making their way through dark, confined spaces filled with sharp rocks and muddy water.

While Hodges was looking up at the mud lines, Anderson looked down and worried. When they arrived at the cave at two in the morning, the water had been ankle deep. Within an hour it had reached two feet. He thought the cave was "undiveable." As the day went on, seven inches of rain poured from the sky.

Diver Ben Reymenants, a charming and gregarious person with many Thai friends, heard that the British divers had arrived and did not think he was needed. Then Ruengrit Changkwanyuen, who had arrived with the Thai singer early on, told him that the Thai SEALs could use support. Reymenants agreed, and flown from his diving school in southern Thailand to the site by AirAsia along with his eighty-five pounds of tanks, masks, and wet suits, he joined the growing throng at the cave.

Everyone knew that if any of the boys or Ek were still alive, they must be past the T-junction, somewhere above the water. Cave explorers reported that Pattaya Beach and a smaller sandy ledge past that would probably stay dry even as the caves flooded and would probably have enough oxygen to let people breathe; water dripping down would be naturally filtered as it drained through the stalactites, keeping it clear and safe to drink. The challenge, the necessity, was to cross the junction. But two streams of water met there, making the current prohibitively strong. Even entering the cave was difficult. Reymenants had to fight against the current, pulling himself along the rope line with his heavy gear, inching forward in caverns growing ever smaller. As Stanton described it, half of the cave system was totally underwater and half was like swimming against the current in a canal. This was the beast the divers would have to master to reach the boys.

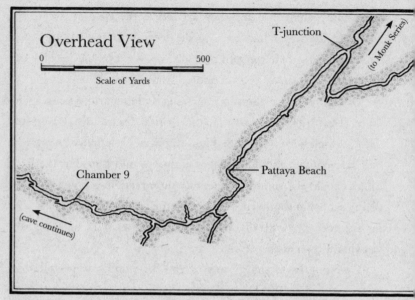

0   500

Scale of Yards

T-junction

(to Monk Series)

Chamber 9

Pattaya Beach

(cave continues)

The rushing waters at the T-junction prevented the divers from discovering the team's fate.

Thursday, June 28

A second day of seven inches of rain was filling the caves. Just as the international helpers began their work, a new crisis arose. Srivara Rangsibrahmanakul, a high-ranking Thai police official, arrived at the cave and told them they would all be in trouble unless they requested and received permission from him to be there. He claimed to be protecting a national park, but in fact he was making himself important and putting a stop to the rescue. The chaos at the cave was no longer the press of crowds and the infiltration of thieves:

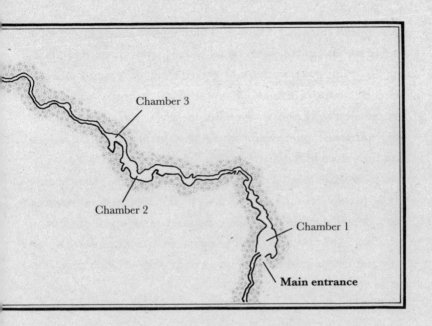

Chamber 3

Chamber 2

Chamber 1

Main entrance

the rescue was a prize for powerful officials to control. Prayut Chan-o-cha, the unpopular retired general who was the prime minister of Thailand, won respect by telling the police official to leave and the rescuers to continue. Even as personal egos and political conflicts dominated the outside of the cave, conditions inside were growing ever more treacherous.

Stanton and Volanthen made one attempt to reach the T-junction, but the dirty, turbulent water was too difficult even for them and they turned back. On their second trip they reached Chamber Three. Earlier, the Thai SEALs and other workers had managed to enter that chamber to stash reserve gas tanks and food, and to set up a place for the giant water pumps. Long tubes looking like giant brown worms now snaked along the ground, carrying water out to the cave mouth. Supposedly everyone had managed to get out after stocking the caves. But the divers came upon the four frightened water pump workers mentioned in the prologue. The men had been stuck in the chamber for a full day—trapped by flows that had risen while they worked. Two flooded segments—sumps, each about twenty feet long and filled with cool water—stood between the men and a scramble to safety. Each section was just too long to cross by holding your breath. The men couldn't stay, as water would only rise farther and flood more sections; they couldn't dive; they could not escape.

The divers made an instant decision: they would dive the men out in relays, using the tanks and breathing apparatus available in the cave. Each cave diver strapped two canisters to his side, with regulators to manage the flow of air to himself and his cargo. *Snatch and grab.* Clutching the guide rope in one hand, the diver hugged a worker with the other, gave each a mouthpiece linked to gas, and dove into the water. All the way across it was an "underwater wrestling match" as the workers thrashed in the water—yet ultimately held on, "keen to get out." One by one, the men made it across, and the British divers learned two opposing lessons.

The chaos of the rescue effort had left four men behind, trapped. The water was now moving so quickly, and was so littered with dirt and debris, that it was like swimming through dense fog. Not even Stanton and Volanthen could safely navigate in it. Trying again was

As hundreds and then thousands of people came to the cave, police tried to establish order.

likely to lead to two horrible outcomes: rescuers would be killed and everyone, the thousands gathered at the cave, would remain there, helpless. With every effort blocked by the water, mothers, fathers, classmates, friends, officials, SEALs, volunteers would know that they were all just waiting for the inevitable end. The two divers considered leaving, going home rather than remaining for that awful vigil. Instead they chose to stay. For, should conditions change, there was a flicker of hope: in saving the four water pump workers, they learned that even in such a dangerous cave, with people who had no diving experience, a rescue might be possible.

5

"Empty the Water Here"
Friday and Saturday, June 29–30

Friday, 3:00 p.m.
INSIDE

BEN REYMENANTS WAS NOT EVEN SURE HE COULD SAVE HIS OWN life. He and his diving partner tried to reach the T-junction. When he finally made it back to his base, he met Stanton and Volanthen. "This is madness," Reymenants said. "We have to call it off, because it is not going to happen. People will die, and we don't even know if those kids are alive." The British divers agreed. With this current, the rains, and the ever-rising water, diving was simply suicide.

Reymenants gave the bad news to the Thai Navy SEAL commander. He could not, would not, accept their judgment. "These boys are from Thailand," the Belgian diver heard him say. "I can't face the public and say, 'We're calling it off.' I'm going to send in my Navy SEALs and we're going to try."

The experienced cave divers knew that further dives would be a terrible, tragic mistake. The SEALs were young men, some even teenagers, who had never tackled caves. Sending them into the raging currents and jagged rocks would be murder.

OUTSIDE

Friday was the third consecutive day of five to seven inches of rainfall. Staff Sergeant Michael Galindo had landed in Thailand the day before with Major Hodges. After a short rest, he set about hiking through the dense tangle of trees and vines in the jungle-covered hills above the flooded cave system. Then he had a piece of luck: he found a gap, dropped a line, and was able to rappel down into a "massive cavern." Perhaps this would be an alternative entrance for rescuers, or an exit for whoever was alive in the cave. As he explored, though, the sergeant saw that the space was cut off at both ends by boulders. Hand over hand, he pulled himself up and out.

One pathway blocked.

The skilled cave divers had called a halt to dives on Thursday. Even the Thai SEAL captain reported that inside the caverns the "noise was deafening." The sound, that is, of flood waters rushing through the system.

A second pathway blocked.

Despite the focused efforts of the best rescue teams and cave divers in the world, the twelve boys and their coach were sealed into the cave. "Everyone," Governor Osottanakorn admitted, "is discouraged." The Thai press reported that some parents were losing hope and in tears, while others were unable to sleep, or having fainting spells requiring medical attention. Yet there was also a tone of optimism and trust in at least what most stated publicly. "I was shocked and crying in Bangkok," one parent said. "I got on the plane and arrived here in the morning. I haven't slept since. I have trust in the rescue officers to do everything in their ability to rescue the kids; at any rate, right now I just want them to be out of the cave. Everything else comes after that. I am confident the kids will survive—they are athletes, I have faith in their strength."

Perhaps it was the very combination of dread and a wish to believe in the power of the rescuers that reached the Thai leadership. General Prayut Chan-o-cha, who had overruled the intrusive police official, arrived to support and encourage the workers and the families. Parents placed their trust in the government. But that also meant the government could be judged on the team's fate. Whether all, some—or worse, none—of the team was found alive, every possible resource would be used. Twenty-four hours a day, hundreds of Thai police officers, SEALs, water workers, and volunteers were devoted to the task.

Governor Osottanakorn understood the risks the moment held for everyone. He told the Thai rescue team that if any of them found conditions too dangerous, they were free to leave with no judgment or blame. He did not want even the brave, trained Thai SEALs to put their lives in danger. But he asked those who remained to see the boys as their own children. He was the kind of leader who is blunt and fair and inspires everyone to give their best through caring and concern, not fear. And ever more help kept arriving.

On Friday seven members of the Beijing Peaceland Foundation arrived at the cave from Zimbabwe carrying five hundred ropes, an underwater robot, GPS monitors, and other equipment. At first the Thais, Americans, and Australians were hesitant about what part these volunteers could play. But as the Chinese showed their experience and expertise, they were welcomed as part of the team. On Saturday five more Chinese, these from the Green Boat Emergency Rescue Alliance, reached the cave. They joined Thai and Palestinian volunteers hacking their way through the hilltop jungles, looking for new ways into the caverns. As the Palestinians worked with the Chinese, an Israeli diver who lived in Thailand arrived on the scene with his son to offer their help.

Some ten thousand people from all over Thailand and across the globe were now at the cave. There may have been hints of tensions between divers and competition among nations. Yet everyone knew that those frictions did not matter at all. The ever more massive effort to find a way through the hills kept yielding promising leads, which, like the sergeant's cavern, proved to be dead ends.

The American rescue team grabbed their chain saws and set about clearing a helicopter landing site so drills could be flown to the hills and used to carve down through the limestone. Yet even once the drills were in place, an impossible challenge would remain: knowing where to aim them. There were no recent, precise maps of the caverns. A hole drilled too close to the boys might endanger them, and too far would be useless. Since the rescuers could only guess where the team must be if they were alive, placing the drill hole correctly would be much closer to blind luck than skill. But with

This image gives a sense of the difficult conditions all the rescue workers faced. The team at work here are the Chinese Peaceland Foundation crew.

the halt to diving, more and more people were sent to scour the hills.

The key to everything was water. The last three days of continuous and heavy rains had stopped the divers. Larger and larger pumps were now pulling millions of gallons of water out of the caves. Yet even as those torrents flooded out, it was not enough to make the caves safe to dive.

Deep in the Cave

Teaching the boys to meditate was one gift—a survival technique— Ek was able to offer them. Another was chores. He set the team to scraping, digging, trying to gouge out a pathway through the walls. No one discussed how far they might have to dig or whether this would or could work. The effort provided a focus. Ek and the boys created a rotation: whenever diggers began to flag, a new set who had been resting and gathering their strength replaced them.

The work rotation Ek created served two purposes: over the long haul, digging might help them escape, and moment to moment, it gave each person a sense of purpose—a reason to have hope. As the dark hours and days went by, older team members looked out for younger ones, encouraging them, helping them to keep up their spirits. Drink, meditate, dig, rest—they were in danger but they were together, guided by Ek—whom they were now so close to they called him "brother," not "coach." The Wild Boars were trapped in the darkness, but they were a band of brothers helping one another— and doing their best.

A sound, a whistle—they heard it, once. The whistle told the boys something they had believed all along: Adults knew they were missing and were on the way, trying to find them. The boys trusted Ek and adults like him. Their job was to be calm and healthy—and to think about soccer. The World Cup was taking place, and the boys had strong favorites. Talking about the matchups, the pairings, that were probably taking place kept them engaged. Meditate, work, listen, trust, talk: minutes, hours, days passed.

Far away in Chile, Omar Reygadas, a miner who in 2010 had been trapped 2,300 feet underground for sixty-nine days with thirty-two other men, knew exactly what the team was experiencing. He thought the coach was the key, for if through humor, prayer, and group activity he could keep up their spirits, that would make all the difference. Alberto Iturra Benavides, a psychologist who had worked with the miners in Chile, added his own insight. "It's valuable for them to be occupied and have tasks to be responsible for within their group—small chores . . . having a set schedule with activities . . . All of this should be on a rotating basis." Small chores, a firm but rotating schedule—if you substitute meditation for prayer, Ek was doing precisely what experts and miners had discovered to be the keys to survival. If, that is, they could be found in time. The more the caves filled with water, the less oxygen remained in the air.

Saturday, June 30

A break in the weather came, and the rains ebbed and then stopped. The water pumps were working too, which created a new set of volunteers. Fields belonging to 101 rice farmers were drowned under the rivers spilling out of the pumps. None of the farmers minded. Indeed, Sri Tammachoke, a farmer whose round face and soft words suggest kindness, depth, and unwavering certainty, explained that she could not eat or sleep so long as the boys were lost. "Empty the water here," she urged. "If the water reached the children, they would be dead. If the paddy fields were flooded, we could replant the rice." When the Thai government offered to compensate the farmers and provide new seeds for a fresh crop, she refused. "I felt bad for the government," she explained. "They spent a lot of money already."

Teams of Thai SEALs—who had been given quick instructions in cave diving—now entered the cave in waves to stash supplies in

Chamber Three. Getting there—even before reaching the forbidding T-junction—was a set of diving, crawling, and rock climbing challenges. Built by nature, not humans, the caves were like a combination of a maze and an amusement park fun house. No step was like the last: one moment you could splash across rocks with water at your ankles, the next you needed to dive, a third to climb, and always your only light was the lamp on your helmet. All you could see was a glancing bloom of bright white, illuminating walls made up of sharp rocks pointing like sharpened wedges. No step was safe.

Sergeant Galindo described the journey to Chamber Three, step by treacherous step. Leaving his staging area, he had to walk for about five minutes carrying several thirty-five-pound scuba tanks on his back to reach the cave entrance. Edging down slippery steps made out of muddy sandbags, he managed the thirty-degree slope into the dark water, a headlamp his only guide. The sergeant dove the ten-to-fifteen-foot gap until he reached a rope that would help him climb up. But the passage was so narrow and filled with stalactites that to avoid hitting his head or risking his gas tanks he had to turn upside down, pulling his way along the rope while hanging below it. The rope landed him in Chamber One, where he had a short walk in a tight space. By the time he got there, water levels had gone down even farther than when the first Thai SEALs made the trip. But that only meant that he marched along through water at shoulder level until he reached the next thirty-foot flooded area where he needed to dive. That swim allowed him to reach a three-foot-high space in which he crawled on his hands and knees. Finally he reached the massive cavern of Chamber Two.

Galindo arrived there wet, muddy, dehydrated, and ready for the final passage. Along the right side of the cavern was a tight path guarded by boulders, which he had to squeeze through and climb over, finding a way up, down, and finally across. This earned him access to a narrow "chimney" that he could just slide up, if he went slowly and carefully enough. His next dive took him across another ten to fifteen feet until he reached the slippery slope into Chamber Three. This snaking obstacle course was only the preface, the easy part, before the real, dangerous diving began.

As soon as the water levels were low enough to make this trip possible, the Thai SEALs began filling Chamber Three with supplies. Over several days they managed to bring in about a hundred gas canisters, tents, lights, food, even KFC fried chicken. As their commander explained, "We had to dive, we had to walk, we had to climb through stone and rock, but we had to keep fighting. If we did not keep moving forward, there would not be hope for the children." The base camp in Chamber Three meant that the expert cave divers could once again attempt to lay line up to and across the T-junction and reach the boys.

6

"How Many?"
Sunday and Monday, July 1–2

Sunday, July 1
INSIDE

ON SUNDAY THREE TEAMS OF DIVERS WERE BACK IN THE WATER laying line from where operations had halted the previous day. Each pair would need to swim out laying line, then return. Because so much of the cave system was now flooded, they had to begin at Chamber Three and travel the entire route. Reymenants and the French diver Maksym Polejaka went first and reached somewhere between Chambers Four and Five. A pair of Thai SEAL divers took the next shift. Then Stanton and Volanthen finally managed to reach the T-junction but did not yet attempt to cross it—they had run out of line. What Stanton calls "the tricky navigational bit" lay just past where the two streams joined. The current flowing down the Monk Series was clearer and noticeably warmer than the current coming from the passage to Pattaya Beach, and beyond, which was muddy and close to 73 degrees Fahrenheit (23 degrees Celsius)—the same as the overall temperature of the main cave. The British team were wearing thin and frayed wet suits that offered little warmth, but they were used to these conditions, and considered them comfortable.

OUTSIDE, 8:30 P.M.

The Chinese Green Boat team got the most exciting, most urgent phone call. One of the rescuers combing the hills had heard a tapping coming from underground. Were the boys alive? Had they managed to make so much noise that it could be heard even through the rock? Could this be a kind of code rumbling from inside the limestone prison? The Chinese rescuers rushed out into the night, thrashing through the pineapples, scampering up cliffs, following a Thai guide. Scraped by sharp leaves, battered by falls, they pressed on but did not find anything. They were not even sure they were in the right place. The team checked back with the original caller, and when they compared GPS locations found out they were miles off target. Indeed, there was no real target. The sound was not the echo of the boys scraping at the rocks but a river rushing through the caves. Discouraged, the Chinese returned to their camp to rest and recover.

Monday, July 2
INSIDE

Leading off the day's dives, Reymenants and Polejaka followed the line the British team had laid on Sunday afternoon. The British team had reached to within 30 feet (9 meters) of that difficult point just

Rick Stanton entering the cave. The lamps and cameras on his helmet guided his way and recorded the journey.

past the T-junction. This, as Stanton describes it, was like being at "a cross roads with additional blind exits, plus all exits being at differing levels to each other." The two divers crossed through the puzzling space and laid about another 377 feet (115 meters) of line. That put them at the same point where the SEALs had left their marker in the early days. The team attached their line and swam back.

Now the British divers left Chamber Three and began the long swim. To handle these difficult dives, some used a special apparatus called a "rebreather," which allows a diver to go longer on a single canister. But Stanton and Volanthen didn't want the additional drag against the current that came with the bulkier equipment.

Stanton and Volanthen reached the T-junction and made their way through the cross roads and blind exits. They reached the end of Reymenants's rope and the SEALs' sign. They were making progress—but that also meant they were coming to the end. It is one thing to be blocked from entering a cave where people are lost. It is another to be swimming closer, hour by hour, minute by minute, to learning their fate.

According to one diver, the Thais wanted to ensure that the last push would be led by a Thai medic who could speak with the team and assess their conditions. William Stone, the cave rescue expert, has said that when there is a search whose every step is covered by the hungry media, there is always tension over the "trophy." Whoever makes the final discovery gets the press, the attention, the praise for his or her nation. As the divers pressed on, someone would, and someone wouldn't, be that person. If you cared about the trophy, the winner would soon be decided. But even for those who didn't, diving onward brought new pressures.

Images haunted Volanthen's and Stanton's minds—they kept picturing the boys swept up, overcome, drowned by the tidal surges. Around the next corner might be thirteen floating bodies. In 2012 Stanton received a high honor—the Member of the Most Excellent Order of the British Empire (MBE)—for trying to find and save

Rick Stanton (*left*) and John Volanthen (*right*). Once it was possible to cross the T-junction, divers knew they would very soon learn the fate of the team.

the French diver Eric Establie, who was lost in a cave. Stanton was only able to recover Establie's body. Volanthen recalled leaving for another dive with three people in a car and returning with two. They were realists navigating the darkness. Every time they sensed an air pocket above the water they would raise their heads out and look, afraid of what they might see.

The divers reached and passed Pattaya Beach. Nothing. No sign of Ek and the team. They swam on, laying line; one hundred meters, two hundred, three hundred, four hundred, five hundred. They were running out of rope. Very soon, for their own safety, they would need to turn around, go back.

An air pocket. Stanton raised his head to look around, then took off his face mask to sniff the air for any trace of human scent. Until now, water rushing through the caves had kept the air clear. The smell was overwhelming—like an outhouse. Someone was here, or had been here.

"There they are," he said. "We've found them!"

Found whom? Found what? The odor said people *had* been here.

Silence.

No sounds.

No sign of the team.

The Team

One shift was doing its work scraping at the rocks when they heard something, voices. Ek told everyone to be silent so they could listen. The boys went still.

Yes, they were right. They were hearing voices, conversation.

Adul grabbed a flashlight and came down the wedge of sand to see who, what, was in the water.

The Divers

Volanthen swam closer, the camera on his helmet filming. Stanton was scanning the steep sandy slope and keeping a tally of the boys. One by one the boys and Ek were rounding a bend out of the darkness and edging down the thin wedge of slope toward the light.

Contact

"How many of you?" Volanthen asked.

"They're all alive!" Stanton exclaimed—his count had told him that already.

"Thirteen," Adul—the one team member who spoke English—replied.

"Brilliant."

The boys began speaking to one another in Thai as Adul and Volanthen exchanged words in English.

Thank you; thank you. Outside?

Not today; just two of us; you have to dive.

(The diver says "not today.")

We're coming, it's okay. Many people are coming;

many, many people. We are the first.

What day?

Tomorrow.

No, what day is it?

Monday.

(Who can speak English? Please help to translate.)

Monday. But one week, Monday. You have been here

ten days. You are very strong. Very strong. We come.

We come.

We are hungry.

I know. I understand.

Eat. Eat. We haven't eaten at all.

We come here tomorrow; we hope tomorrow. Navy

SEALs will come tomorrow with food and doctors and

everything. Have a light? We'll give you more lights.

We are happy.

We are happy too.

Thank you so much. Where are you from?

England, the UK.

Beyond all hope, all thirteen were alive—very thin, all bones and knobby knees, but smiling, seemingly healthy and in good spirits. But from the first second, the divers realized that they were facing a new crisis: how could they possibly get these skeletal young men out?

For two of the very best, most experienced cave divers in the world, the trip from the base camp had taken two and a half hours of squeezing, wiggling, navigating through tight, treacherous caverns. Could thirteen frail young men with no diving experience at all, much less cave diving under the most hazardous conditions, undertake that journey?

That night six Thai SEALs and Dr. Pak Loharnshoon—who had received SEAL training but became an army doctor—equipped with four oxygen tanks each set out to follow the five-hour round trip from Chamber Three to the boys and back. Five hours passed, six, eight, nine. Twenty-three hours later three SEALs returned, totally exhausted. They had each used three tanks just to reach the boys, so only a few were willing to chance coming back on a single tank. SEALs in peak physical condition could barely complete the dive. As cave diver Jason Mallinson put it, getting thirteen people out of the cave would not be difficult; getting them out alive was another challenge entirely.

At nine thirty that night, Governor Osottanakorn was holding

A beaming Governor Osottanakorn addressing the press at the cave mouth on July 4. The team had been found, and all efforts were focused on planning for the rescue.

an important, difficult meeting. Meteorologists were reporting that worse weather, an even bigger storm was on the way. The boys and Ek had been gone for ten days. For ten days the governor had done everything he could to give people hope, to rally their spirits, to encourage them to trust. But ten days was a long time to go without food, and if the new storm made the caves even more impassible, how could the boys survive? What could the governor and his team possibly say to everyone tomorrow?

A Thai SEAL arrived and asked the governor to step out of the meeting. He had news: the boys had been found, and they were all alive! Governor Osottanakorn was not sure whether to trust the news. But he decided he could not take the time to confirm the story.

Instead, he sought out the parents and told them "we found your kids, healthy, alive." Then at ten p.m., he made the announcement to the world. The press burst into cheers.

Major Hodges and his team immediately realized that their mission had totally changed. Searching outside across the hills was over. Now all their attention must be on the chambers and passages within the caves. He and his key people rushed to the cave mouth to meet the British divers and Thai SEALs and plan.

7

"This Is Our Best Shot"

Tuesday-Wednesday-Thursday-Friday, July 3–6

FINDING THE TEAM HAD MEANT SOLVING THREE PROBLEMS: drying out the caves, bringing the best divers, and combing the hills for new entrances. Now that the thirteen had been located, three possible plans emerged for bringing them out. The first, which was the most cautious and perhaps the safest, was to leave them where they were, ferrying in food, medicines, and company for four months until the rainy season ended. Then they could easily walk or be carried out across what would, by then, be well-trodden dry passages.

Unsworth thought this was madness. Seeing how nearly impassible the caverns had been at the start of the rainy season, what would they be like later on? How could anyone be sure that enough supplies would reach the team before they were sealed in by the water? What if someone got sick or developed an infection after the rains cut them off? Yet others disagreed. For now the caverns could be dived and supplies could be stored. The rains were seasonal. They would eventually end. And when they did, exiting the cave would not be hazardous at all. It would be hard for the team and their families to wait, but they would have no reason to worry about how everyone would get out.

A second idea was to keep up the search for a pathway down through the limestone hills. That would mean neither having to wait out the rain nor risking an extremely difficult diving exit when the boys were still so weak. Yet the hundreds, even thousands, of people walking the hills, assisted by local guides, birds' nest collectors, national parks rescue teams, policemen, Thai soldiers, the Chinese Green Boat Alliance—even detailed topological maps of the terrain helpfully beamed down from a Japanese satellite—were getting nowhere.

The third choice was to dive the team out right away. But a cave rescue that required bringing thirteen people, including a child as young as eleven, none of them divers, 1.5 miles (2.4 kilometers) through a cave system that, when flooded, is considered one of the most dangerous in the world, was infinitely beyond anything that had ever been attempted. Mallinson, who comes across as blunt and tough-minded, was very skeptical. His "first thought" was "that they're not going to get out. It's all about panic underwater. You can tell a kid whatever you want. But in an actual situation, if you've got a kid underwater, more than likely they're going to panic. So at first we thought it's not possible to dive them out." The chances of complete success—bringing all thirteen plus every diver out alive—were grim. Going with this choice would decide the issue right away, one way or the other. Yet the families would know that their children, now smiling, alive, sending their love, might very well lose their lives in the attempt.

And the clock was ticking—more rains were predicted. A Thai geologist and a Japanese irrigation specialist each realized that there was a new way to think about the water problem. The irrigation specialist, Hideki Furihata, told a Japanese newspaper, "It's important to drain water from the cave, but it's equally important to stop the water from entering." If one could figure out where most of the water was coming from, one might be able to divert the streams before they flooded the caverns. The geologist, Chaiporn Siripornpibul, managed to determine at least three sources and, working with the Japanese irrigation specialist, redirected them. While pumps could help to dry out areas from Chamber Three to the entrance, diversion could lower water levels deeper in the cave, creating some spots where rescuers could walk on dry land. So long as there were no new rainstorms, the diversion would buy the rescuers a little time.

In Australia two members of the Wet Mules cave-diving team—Dr. Richard "Harry" Harris and Craig Challen, a retired veterinary surgeon—were packed and about to go on a vacation trip. Stanton texted Harris, who was internationally known as an expert cave diver with specialized medical training, to ask him to take part in an impossible plan. Harris is an anesthesiologist, and Stanton wanted him to dive out to the boys and then, when it came time, to put them to sleep one by one so they would be unconscious through the rescue. Harris texted back that that was a crazy idea, but he and Challen would come to the cave to see for themselves. Harris and

Challen had forty-five minutes to unpack, repack, and head off to catch a flight to Thailand. From what they knew so far, the prospects of a successful rescue were, as Challen said, "bleak."

SEAL divers assisted by retired SEALs began shifts of diving into Chamber Three with three tanks on their backs and three trailing behind. From Three, the other divers took the extra tanks to key spots along the route. The more well-stocked resupply stations there were, the easier to convoy food and medicine to the Wild Boars and to prepare supplies to assist in the rescue. Though the experienced cave divers were managing to navigate the passages, the treacherous trips required total, constant attention. Mallinson explained:

"You are swimming against the current on the way in, so usually the visibility is not too bad. It is usually fine for the first divers, but the first diver is finning, and that creates eddies in the water, which stirs up the silt and then the second diver doesn't get such good visibility, and then the third diver gets even worse. So by the time you've got a fifth or a sixth diver in there, you're down to nil visibility. And then when you get to the end of the cave and you turn around and come out, you are with the current, so anything you stir up at the end of the cave is going to flow all the way out with you, so you tend to have a much worse visibility on the way out. It's a bit of a combat course on the way out. Sometimes you can only just feel the line. Sometimes you can see a foot in front of you. Other times it's just nothing, it's all by braille. It's quite a mentally exhausting experience."

The cave mouth in the dry season.

This color image from the 1984 Peña Colorada exploration gives a sense of the beauty and mystery that captivates cave divers.

The cave filled with rescue teams.

Endless lines of hose needed to be brought into the cave to bring out the water and allow divers to try to cross the T-junction.

Hoses, looking like streamers, lined up to bring water out of the cave.

As pumps filled the hoses, they became pipes carrying water to farmers' rice paddies.

Even when they didn't need to dive, rescue teams worked in water that could reach anywhere from their ankles to their chests.

One of the boys in the cave, taken the day after Rick Stanton and John Volanthen reached the team.

Wearing their Mylar coverings to keep warm, the team members were still weak and hungry, but eager to tell the world they were okay.

The last phase of the rescue: Thai Navy SEALs bringing one of the team on a Sked out of the cave.

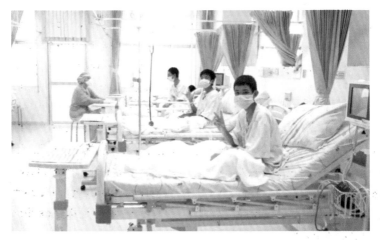

The team resting and recovering in the hospital.

At the press conference, the team, along with Ek and the governor, recounted their impossible story.

Wednesday

Harris reached the cave and swam out to the boys. He realized he had been wrong. "Once I had dived the cave myself I could see that it would be impossible to dive the kids out in any other way except asleep, because it was a pretty tricky cave, was pretty tight, zero visibility a lot of the time." He knew that "to ask an eleven-year-old boy to just close his eyes, trust me and come for a three-hour swim in that environment, it's just not going to happen. He would panic in the first ten minutes and would drown." But now he and Challen faced another dilemma: they were trying to figure out whether, as Challen put it, "sedation or anesthesia could possibly be done without killing the lot of them."

"An offer of help came from an unexpected source: Elon Musk. Musk is the innovative billionaire businessman responsible for the Tesla car and the SpaceX exploration company. Between Musk's large budget and the staff of highly skilled engineers at his disposal, it was just possible that he could find a way to diminish the terrible risks ahead.

Thursday: Chamber Nine

The three Thai SEALs and Dr. Pak were now living out on the sandy bank with Ek and the boys. Ek began to see the SEALs as "like family." One SEAL in particular—unusually, his name, Baitei, was made public—took on a special role. "Baitei felt like a father to me," one Wild Boar said. In turn, the SEAL began calling each of the players "son." Just as the team had felt Ek's protection during their dark, isolated days, they now experienced Baitei as a guiding,

Thai Navy SEALs worked tirelessly to bring supplies into the cave.

comforting parent. Baitei managed to bring a version of chess with him and taught his newfound family to play. Several players began thinking that they would like to train to become SEALs when they grew up. Even as the team and their SEALs bonded, other SEALs were busy ferrying gas tanks and supplies through the caves. Four divers, two Thai and two foreign, set off on a five-hour round trip oxygen run.

Friday

1:30 A.M.

SEAL captain Surawan was still in Chamber Three, waiting. The divers had been gone for more than thirteen hours. Finally one diver emerged, saying his buddy was near but out of oxygen. Minutes later the body of retired Navy SEAL Lieutenant Commander Saman Gunan was fished out of the water. How he died is still a mystery. Divers, even those who were on the scene in the cave, cannot piece together what took place. He should have been diving with a partner who could have saved him. Perhaps he hit his head—most of the volunteer divers did not have protective helmets. Or perhaps some deadly gas had gotten into his tank.

Gunan's death highlighted the grave danger of using the SEALs—whose dive training had been entirely in open water—in the treacherous caves. He was fit, brave, and had been a skilled diver, though he had retired from the SEALs twelve years earlier. But the caves were absolutely unforgiving. However, he lost consciousness, and as he thrashed about in the dark water, his chances of survival dropped with each second, until it was too late.

The thirty-seven-year-old retired SEAL did not need to be in the cave. As his wife recalled, he loved doing charity work and being of help to other people. That is why he chose to come to help rescue the Wild Boars and to assist his fellow SEALs. Governor Osottanakorn called him "the hero of the Tham Luang Cave." He was a hero. The motto of the American pararescue team is "that others may live." They train for years to be willing to risk, even to give up, their own lives to save a fallen soldier—or a trapped Thai soccer team. Though he was from a different nation, Lieutenant Commander Saman Gunan exemplified that motto.

Everyone was stunned by the death—which only made the mission all the more urgent. If they all gave their all, if they could succeed, then at least his death would not have been in vain. And as divers shuttled to and from the team, they realized that there was a silent, deadly threat in the air.

Water still filled much of the cavern where the team had found shelter. Now the thirteen Wild Boars plus four rescuers who were keeping them company were sharing the tight space. High water, people, confined space, limited air, is not a good combination. The air should be 20 percent oxygen, and as of now it was 15 percent. If that number dropped below 13 percent, everyone would begin to experience the same kind of disorientation that may have befallen Gunan. By 10 percent they would faint, and at 6 percent they would die. More oxygen could be pumped in—if a pipe could be snaked all the way from the mouth of the cavern. But it proved impossible to bring the pipe past Chamber Three. Oxygen tanks were being opened in the chambers to release more oxygen into the air and to fight the rising levels of carbon dioxide, but they could never do enough. Diversion could temporarily hold back the water, but there was no obvious way to save the air.

Musk had sent his engineers to the cave and was working out ideas for assisting. But what these plans would be, whether they could be completed in time, and whether they would work, was anyone's guess.

The American leaders—Hodges and Anderson—along with the Thai SEAL commander, reached a decision. They could not leave the team in the cave, and they could not keep hoping another entrance would be found. There was only one choice, the very worst choice: dive the team out now.

9:00 P.M.

The Americans rushed to meet with the highest Thai leaders—the governor, admirals, the minister of the interior. Hodges faced the moment he knew might come: he would have to convince the Thai government—which had the eyes of all Thailand watching it—to approve a plan that he expected would result in losses of life. The cave had claimed one victim already. He gave his honest assessment—there was only a 60 to 70 percent chance of success. To put those numbers more starkly, he expected that three, four, even five young people would not survive the trip.

"We either have a shot where we could get some of them out," Anderson insisted, "or we leave 'em in there and there's a very, very high chance that none of 'em survive." He added, speaking as forcefully as he could, "This is our best shot." Would the government, which would be blamed if children died, be willing to take the risk? Hodges made a direct plea: he knew that emotions were running high, but in a crisis such as this, "emotions are not your friend." Would this blunt American style upset the more gracious, diplomatic Thais? Just the opposite. Hodges sensed that the Thai leaders were glad the Americans had been so brutally honest, for that took the question out of their hands. The Thai government agreed that there was no choice, no chance to wait. They would have to risk the impossible rescue.

8

The Impossible Rescue
Saturday, July 7

IF THE WINDING, HAZARD-FILLED CAVE SYSTEM, THE MUDDY current, and the enveloping darkness were the enemies, there was only one way to defeat them: the most meticulous planning, along with complete international cooperation. The expert cave divers could navigate safely by themselves, but in order to bring out the team, they would need precisely organized support at every step of the journey. Every single individual involved, no matter which nation he hailed from or what language he spoke, must know, accept, and execute his job. The only way to obtain that total agreement and total commitment was through the open exchange of ideas.

Major Hodges and his team developed one plan, the Thai military another. The groups consulted, adjusted, developed a joint vision. The British divers, and now an Australian team, were invited in. Even though they were a civilian voluntary rescue group, the

Chinese from the Beijing Peaceland Foundation felt welcomed, included, and treated as equals. As one told a Chinese reporter, "They took care of our emotions and took the initiative to ask the Chinese team's opinions when formulating the plan. They actively praised our team for being excellent." This attentive care did not mean everyone agreed from the beginning, only that everyone felt seen, appreciated, and heard.

A map was needed: the planners must have a guide in order to give everyone their assignments. They could rely only on a thirty-year-old French survey. Stanton used that to sketch out a simplified diagram of the cave system on a whiteboard (see photo on page 77 of Zhou Yahui in front of that very map). The first four chambers were defined in the survey, so he then made up Chambers Five, Six, and Seven to space out the journey, and that served as everyone's guide. Dr. Martin Ellis tried a different approach, which did not end up being utilized. Dr. Ellis, an authority on Thai caves who had explored the Tham Luang system with Unsworth and Harper, sent further information, and a team of geographers from the Thai Department of Mineral Resources compiled a 2-D and then a 3-D model of the cave.

Given the map and using the whiteboard, team leaders drew diagrams of the cave system and mapped out who would need to be where with which resources. At every step, planning needed to be in duplicate: Who would do what if the rescue was going well? Could there be a backup in case of failure or emergency? Between the sandy spot where now seventeen people were gathered and the cave entrance, planners identified nine stations, or chambers, which were above water and could house rescuers. Chamber Three would continue to be the supply point. Old-fashioned walkie-talkies allowed some communication through those first three chambers. The Thais set up a wireless node as well, which the Americans thought was unnecessary, until people began finding WhatsApp to be especially useful.

The first challenge was to create the best possible system for getting material through the obstacle course to the supply center in Chamber Three. The Chinese from the Beijing Peaceland Foundation had special expertise that put them in charge of this assignment. Zhou Yahui knew how to create rope-and-pulley systems under difficult conditions. Working nineteen-hour days in the

Major Charles Hodges, on the far left, and his team meet with a Thai geologist, on the far right, to study maps of the cave and plan the rescue.

Zhou Yahui of the Beijing Peaceland team discusses rescue plans. He is pointing to a map of the cave system with the key chambers labeled and marked. The whiteboard behind him lists the teams assigned to each chamber.

wet caverns, their hands swelling up from constant immersion in water, he and seven coworkers created a "life channel" out of ropes.

The sequence of overhanging ropes guided through pulleys allowed workers to clip on gas canisters and other supplies and haul them into Chamber Three—rather than wrangling them up and down over obstacles and through narrow passages by hand. This sped up the resupply process, and by the end of the first day, some 190 tanks were safely in the chamber. Later on the same Chinese crew had a second assignment. The Thais had already set up a zip line across a steep and slippery hill in Chamber Two. The Chinese

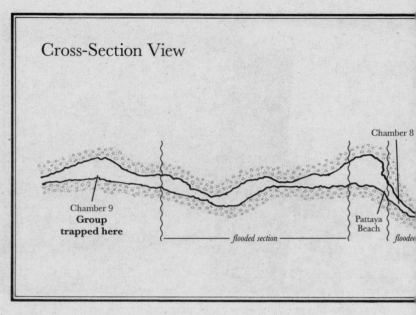

Cross-Section View

Chamber 8

Chamber 9
**Group
trapped here**

Pattaya
Beach

flooded section

floode

This cross-section gives a sense of where the cave system was flooded and where it widened and narrowed.

were asked to help the Thais take it apart and replace it with guide ropes so that, during the rescue, the Wild Boars could be carried hand to hand.

Past Chamber Three the planners faced a second kind of challenge: there would be absolutely no communication. Each chamber was a totally isolated spot separated by water, silence, and complete darkness. No Wi-Fi, no radio, could link them. Rescuers in each chamber would know only as much as they could see and feel right in front of themselves. Disaster plans had to be built assuming no contact from one to another. Rescuers would know the time the

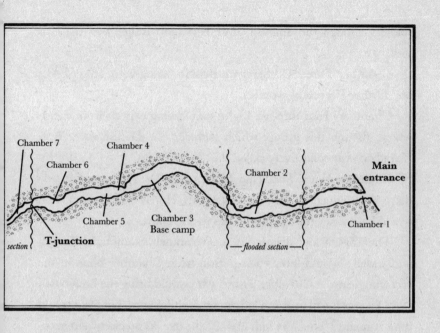

Chamber 7 · Chamber 6 · Chamber 4 · Chamber 5 · Chamber 3 Base camp · Chamber 2 · **Main entrance** · Chamber 1 · **T-junction** · section · *— flooded section —*

mission began, and thus when they might expect to see a diver and a Wild Boar appear in their area. Since the divers would be using the guide ropes the cave divers had laid down as they swam along, rescuers ahead would get a bit of warning about fifteen minutes before a diver appeared—when they would begin to feel tugs on the rope.

The nine chambers would be divided up among the teams, so that rescuers would work with colleagues or associates they could get to know. Workers in each chamber could weigh, consider, envision their specific task.

Chamber One, the cave entrance: the Chinese, Australians, some Americans and Thai navy.

Chamber Two, farther into the cave: Thai SEALs and US

soldiers, though the Spanish diver Fernando Raigal was there as well.

Chamber Three: US Sergeant Brisbin, along with Thai SEALs and further US rescue workers.

Chambers Four through Eight: cave-diving experts from everywhere, though this group, which included the Danish diver Ivan Karadzic, was collectively called the "Euro" team.

Chamber Nine: The Thai SEALs and Dr. Pak were already there, soon joined by the two Australians, Harris and Challen, who would have a key part to play in the rescue effort.

The team of four British divers—Volanthen, Stanton, Mallinson, and Jewell—would ferry each person from Chamber Nine to the receiving team in Chamber Three, who would bring the boys out.

This was the plan as spelled out on a whiteboard, but what would it be in reality? The next step was to rehearse, as precisely and accurately as possible, every action that needed to take place. One way of doing that is what the military calls a "rehearsal of concept" or ROC drill. The ROC drill echoed on a smaller scale the exact layout of the cave, and the men and material in each chamber.

Major Hodges took over a parking lot and chairs were strung together with rope—each one standing for a section of the cave. Water bottles took the place of the gas tanks that would actually be used. A bottle with a green tag was a tank with oxygen measured out to be used by the Wild Boars and Ek; a bottle with a blue tag was air for the divers; bottles marked with red were empty, discarded tanks. In the drill the colors were tags; in the cave the colors would have the same meaning but would come from pads similar to glow sticks. As rescuers paced through the drill, they were like dancers rehearsing by walking through a performance. They were seeing, and beginning to memorize, the actions they would need to take. The ROC drill was also a chance to notice any gaps or bottlenecks.

The Americans spoke in English and there were teams of translators—some paid, some volunteers—there to make sure that everyone knew and understood each step. No matter how many times the rescuers walked through their tasks, though, there was a key piece missing from the rehearsal: the children and teenagers. None of this would work unless the divers could get used to following the guide ropes through the murky water while holding and protecting a young person. And for the Wild Boars to make the dive, the rescuers would need to find diving equipment that would perfectly fit the faces and bodies of eleven-to-seventeen-year-olds.

A local school offered its swimming pool, and Thai students volunteered their services as stand-ins. Each Wild Boar and Ek would be wearing a mask that sealed in his entire face and pumped in the gas mixture he would need to breathe. With a full-face mask there is no need for a mouthpiece; the hose from the tank brings gas to the whole mask. Yet the slightest gap in the mask would let air out and water in, which would first panic and then likely drown the swimmer. Ruengrit Changkwanyuen, who had brought Reymenants to the cave and had arrived with the Thai singer Narinthorn Na Bangchang, was able to find enough full-face masks to go around. But there was a problem—they were designed for adults. At the pool, the Americans put the masks on the middle schoolers and tried adjusting them, one tug on the strap, two, three. With the fifth and

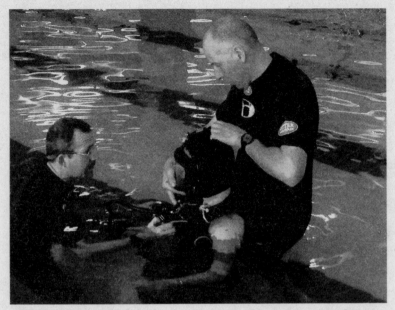

John Volanthon (*left*) and Rick Stanton (*right*) working with a volunteer in a swimming pool to test equipment on a person the same size as the teenaged players.

last pull they were able to close the seal—the masks could just about work. Next came the problem of the water—it would be cold, and the young team members would need to put on wet suits.

The Thai students wriggled into wet suits, the face masks were tightly strapped on, and then they were outfitted with the black buoyancy devices that would help keep them afloat. Now the divers practiced passing along these child-packages over and under water.

As the pool rehearsals went on, Musk and his engineers set about to create what he called "a tiny kid-sized submarine." He thought the device could reach the rescue team by Monday, July 9.

One crucial part of the plan would rest almost entirely on the shoulders of those two Australians, Harris and Challen. The pair had agreed to render all thirteen totally unconscious during the rescue. That would prevent them from falling into the kind of panic Mallinson had predicted and could just make it possible to bring them out safely. The divers made it absolutely clear that they would not undertake the risk if the team members were awake. "I can't have him twitching around," Mallinson explained. "He could have harmed himself. He could have ripped his face mask off and then he was dead." But this would also mean none of the Wild Boars could do anything to save himself. Everything, everything, would depend on the masks staying sealed, the skill of the divers, and the total focus of the international crews in the chambers. The rescue team presented this decision to the Thai authorities, who agreed and accepted total responsibility in case the plan should fail.

Harris and Challen dove out to Chamber Nine to meet the team, to get to know them, and to assess their medical condition. Challen, a hearty, tanned Australian, thought the team was doing well, though he heard the beginnings of coughs or chest infections in a few of them. And he was struck by how small some of the younger players were. Harris had an important message to share. He needed everyone to know that if each one of the Wild Boars and Ek agreed, he would administer the sedative that would put them to sleep for the entire three-hour journey.

Stanton was especially concerned about the smallest boys. Would they be up to the journey? He thought Musk's submarine might be useful for them—if it could be ready and tested in time.

Chamber Nine

The Thai SEALs who had dived out to join the Wild Boars knew that several rescue plans were being discussed. Seeing the players' condition, the SEALs were concerned about asking the team to dive out. "I could only worry," one said, "that diving out might be tough for the kids." Yet even leaving out the danger of the lowering oxygen level and the expected rains, the sandy mound was hardly a comfortable place to stay. Everyone ate, slept, and went to the bathroom in the same tight, humid spot. The smell that had first greeted Stanton was overpowering. It was too hard to get bedding through the caves, so everyone had to sleep on moist, muddy ground.

Still, conditions were improving a bit: The SEALs, Ek, and the boys now had some food—over time about a hundred meals were brought to them through the caverns. Space blankets—the thin Mylar sheets that look like shiny aluminum foil, envelop marathon runners after a race, and help a person retain body heat—kept them warm. Dr. Pak, the Thai medic, was pleased to see that no one had serious wounds or infections, and the few scrapes, cuts, and bruises were swabbed with ointment to make sure they stayed clean and dry. Perhaps most important, though, the team had companionship, and soon, contact with home.

On one of Mallinson's dives, he realized that he was carrying a wet notebook—a pad that you could write on and the words would withstand the trip back. Concerned that not all of the team would make it out safely, he wanted to be sure everyone sent some final word to his parents. As parents read the notes and responded, what had begun out of fear turned into a warm and hopeful exchange.

As a joint note, the team said:

Don't worry, everybody is healthy.
We really want to go out and eat so many types of food.
When we get out, we want to go home right away.
Teacher, don't give us a lot of homework.

Nick was more specific: he sent his love to his parents and his sister. *If I can get out,* he added, *take me to eat crispy pork.*

His parents wrote back: *We've been waiting and still waiting to meet you.*

Bew assured his parents he loved them and promised his mother he would come help out in the store whenever he had free time.

We miss you. Love you always, they replied.

Many parents wrote to say that they would be waiting at the very entrance of the cave.

Ek wrote that the boys were doing well and were getting good care, and that he would do everything for them. And he apologized for having put the team in danger. Parents wrote back to assure him that they were grateful for how thoughtfully he was watching out for their sons.

The team, Ek, and the SEALs were bonding. The British divers arrived on their runs, carrying the same wet suits, masks, and buoyancy jackets that the Thai students had tried on in the swimming pool. Since the Wild Boars would be sedated, they did not need to practice with the equipment. The divers would put it on them, take it off, and be totally responsible for their safety.

The team understood what was about to happen. Since there

were four divers assigned to bringing out the team, four players would go out each day. The team discussed the order—who should go when? They might have chosen by age, or, as in the Chile mine rescue, sent the strongest first—since those in the best shape would be most able to withstand any initial problems. But instead (one story has it), with a kind of delightful optimism, they decided that the Wild Boars should leave in order of how far they would have to travel once they got out. As if this were a dip in a friendly pool, followed by a quick trip home. Some of the Wild Boars actually asked to remain and go last—they so enjoyed spending time with Baitei on their sandy home.

The Thai SEALs had a different understanding of the selection process. They were only certain that the masks they had would form a perfect seal on the faces of the bigger team members. The smallest Wild Boars could not leave until the right equipment for them arrived.

Harris and Challen joined the Wild Boars, Ek, and the SEALs to assess the team and to prepare the way for the final journey.

9

"Fish On"
Sunday-Monday-Tuesday, July 8–10

ON SATURDAY, GOVERNOR OSOTTANAKORN WAS NOT SURE THE Wild Boars were up to risking the trip. Weather forecasts, though, indicated rain was on the way. If water poured down, overwhelming the diversions, overpowering the pumps, and flooding the chambers where rescuers needed to work and supplies were stashed, the one option that had any chance of success would be lost. The rescue, or the tragedy, would begin on Sunday.

Sunday, July 8
CAVE MOUTH, 10:00 A.M.

Mallinson volunteered to bring out the first player. Stanton, Volanthen, and Jewell followed on the three-hour dive to reach the team. In the other chambers, nine more foreign divers, and from Chamber Three to the entrance, five Thai SEALs also had roles to play. Understanding that the rescue was about to begin, the crowd of family, volunteers, friends, and media rushed to the cave. This time, though, the authorities put up a green curtain, masking the cave entrance and separating those essential to the rescue from everyone else. Every reporter, camera operator, and commentator was moved back 1,500 feet (about 450 meters). There was no time for the chaos of the earlier days.

The rescue team added another form of curtain as well—they would not release clear information on which person would come out and when. That way parents would not know when an individual Wild Boar was in danger, or en route. Better that all wait, in hope and fear, together.

Thirteen ambulances parked by the entrance.

CHAMBER NINE

Harris is known for his relaxed, calm, and confident bedside manner. He had gotten to know the team and they trusted him. He explained to each young man that the plan was for him to be asleep throughout the trip, and asked each one for his individual consent. All agreed.

Mallinson arrived. Today, Night, Nick, Note, and Tern were going to risk the journey. The first Wild Boar (WB1) was in his wet suit, fitted with his buoyancy jacket and his full-face mask, and given ketamine, a sedative known to be safe and well-suited to young people, as well as atropine to limit how much saliva he produced so he would not drown himself. The boys were then bound with their hands behind their backs and their feet tied together—to keep them motionless and streamlined. At this point WB1 was a sleeping package. As they slipped into the water, the diver was worried. The very first leg was a long dive—more than a thousand feet (about 350 meters). Every second along the way Mallinson wondered if the mask seal would hold. If it didn't, his only choice would be to swim as fast as he could, to get the sleeping teenager to air, in Chamber Eight. Considering that very possibility, the rescue team had decided to fill all the Wild Boars' gas tanks with 80 percent oxygen. Each sleeping person might have just enough oxygen in his lungs, then, to survive for a few minutes without the mask.

Snatch and Grab: Mallinson was now doing a version of the technique Stanton and Volanthen had used when they rescued the trapped water pump workers from Chamber Three. With one hand he pulled along the guide rope, the line that had been carefully laid throughout all the flooded sections. With his free hand he grasped the handle on the back of the teenager's buoyancy jacket. WB1 was carried along beneath Mallinson face-mask down, so that any water that entered would drain away from his face. The diver must keep his body between the boy and any hanging stalactites, any obstacles that might bump him, dislodge the mask, or dent the equipment.

CHAMBER EIGHT

Mallinson and his living package arrived safely. That was very good news—the seal was holding, the sedative working. Challen and another diver met Mallinson and helped him bring the boy out of the water. Now the three of them needed to carry the sleeping boy across the 450-foot (137-meter) chamber. Finally, at the edge of the chamber, Mallinson slipped into the water and set off again with his sleeping Wild Boar.

Disaster.

WB1 started to stir.

The drug was wearing off. Mallinson took out the extra loaded syringes he had brought, just in case.

In the high water, the syringes began floating away.

Mallinson reached to corral the syringes while searching for his separate store of needles.

Quickly, but without rushing, in the total dark, he needed to hold WB1, find a needle, gather the syringes, administer the dose, return the needles to the dry tube carrying case; and finally, as the boy returned to sleep, Mallinson could swim on. Twice more as he swam, the diver needed to put his stirring passenger back to sleep. Harris had carefully calculated the amount of ketamine to protect the boys, but each dose would last only about forty minutes. That meant that a version of Mallison's adventure would be repeated with every single Wild Boar. While the boys would remain asleep, as the injections wore off, they would become restless, their unseeing eyes would open, and the diver would need to inject them once again.

CHAMBER THREE

Sergeant Brisbin, the one member of the US pararescue team with cave-diving experience, was waiting, reviewing his assignment, making sure he knew exactly what he was to do in every contingency.

Tug. There was a tug on the guideline. Someone was close, no more than a fifteen-minute dive away, and clutching the guide rope

Members of the United States team descend into the cave to take their places in the rescue effort.

as he swam. The team in Chamber Three sent the first WhatsApp message ahead: *Fish on*—"there is a fish on the line," meaning someone was coming.

Mallinson and his sleeping passenger emerged from the water. Sergeant O'Brien rushed to take the teenager out of the diver's hands, turned him over on his side, and listened next to the mask—the boy was breathing. Then he checked his vital signs. "He's good," O'Brien signaled. Now WB1 was bundled into a green plastic rescue stretcher called a Sked, which was attached to the rope-and-pulley system that would carry him over and past the boulders. Thai

SEALs met him there, checked him again, and passed him along to Sergeant Brisbin. He and a partner, Sergeant Merchand, carried WB1 through the sixty-five-foot (twenty-meter) sump—perhaps the same one that Stanton and Volanthen had navigated with the water pump workers—through the chimney to Chamber Two.

Chamber Two was not flooded but presented its own hazards. The Spanish diver Fernando Raigal had arrived on the day the Wild Boars were found and had been part of the crew shuttling from Chamber Three to the T-junction. Now he was part of the team in Chamber Two. Stones littered the ground; there were holes where it would be easy to stumble and waist-high rock formations you could knock into. "Learn the rocks," Raigal had been warned—no need for new accidents.

As the first diver approached, Sergeant Galindo was in the chamber reviewing his assignment. A PJ—a member of the para-rescue team—he had spent two and a half years training to be able to find and recover people from difficult conditions ranging from high mountains and deep sea to urban combat zones. Though his unit's primary mission was to assist downed fighters, he was equally eager to put his skills to use for thirteen people in a Thai cave. He was facing the moment for which he had been preparing for years.

Wrapped tightly in his Sked, the Wild Boar was pulled across one hundred to two hundred feet (thirty to sixty meters) of rope highline from Sergeant Hopper to Sergeant Galindo—within this chamber they had the advantage of being able to communicate by walkie-talkie. Galindo took the Sked off the rope and again did a brief but important check. The teenager was alive, breathing, and had oxygen in his tank. All good. Four men were there, waiting their turn. One man on each corner, they carried the Sked on the fifteen-minute walk to the narrow, very slippery path leading down to Chamber One. Twenty Thai SEALs stood shoulder to shoulder down the thirty-foot (ten-meter) path. They passed WB1 down hand over hand—so there was no chance of him slipping. Waiting at the bottom was a Thai medical crew, ready to make their assessment. Beyond them, in groups stationed about five walking minutes apart, were SEALs who would carry the very first trapped young man out of the cave and into one of the waiting ambulances.

5:40 P.M.

On a day that began with WB1 being sedated in Chamber Nine, he was now alive, safe, and breathing open air. Three more Wild Boars followed with no major mishaps or drama. After each one arrived at Chamber Three, Brisbin checked him and confirmed he was alive, breathing, asleep but unharmed. According to plan, Harris followed the last diver and boy out—just in case. When the diver emerged, a soldier patted him on the shoulder and said, "[F]our out of four, Doc." Harris was so aware of the dangers along every inch of the route that he assumed that meant all of the boys were dead. He could not have been more wrong.

The first day of the impossible rescue had gone impossibly well. But to Hodges, that very success was a danger. He called together the Thai SEALs, the international divers, and the American team for a "hotwash." Like sports coaches watching film of the first game of a championship series, he wanted to review every step, every play. What had gone right, what had gone wrong, what could be improved, what did they have to be alert for that they had missed? "Now is not the time," he warned, "to get complacent or over-confident. . . . We went four for four. We hit a home run, but we can still improve."

The major thought they did not have enough control over who came in and out of the cave, and had not communicated between groups as well as they could have. But he and Anderson thought all the teams should stay together in the same combinations and in the same stations. Challen and the team in Chamber Eight realized that they needed more crew—saving the divers from having to carry the boys—and could take the gear off and put it back on much more quickly. With help, they could save a good deal of time.

Monday, July 9

Overnight the chambers were resupplied. The divers were ready. The team in Chamber Nine was waiting. Today Bew, Dom, Adul, and Mick would go. The weather was dry and the pumps working. Everyone had a day's experience, so they enjoyed a bit more trust that the plan could work.

Planning, training, and the weather held. Four more Wild Boars made it out safely. With the lessons learned from the first day, escape times were reduced to nine and a half hours. Still there was one major challenge ahead: the smallest boys had been held back until the right full-face masks could be brought to them. Stanton was con-cerned about their ability to make the trip and was thinking about the device Musk had promised. Musk himself had reached the cavern and may even have managed to get to Chamber Three. His mini-submarine was delivered and ready. But the international team had experienced two days of success already, and some doubted that the machine was up to the hazards of the cave. The submarine was scheduled to be sent off to the Ministry of Science, and one last time they would trust the masks and the divers.

Outside the cave, the oldest group of Wild Boars, the nineteen-and-under squad, were set to play their first game since their teammates had disappeared. Instead of their normal red and white, the players wore black—in honor of Sergeant Sam. The Mae Sai League Cup was a major tournament for them, as they were one of twenty teams from throughout their region. On that day, even as the American pararescue team, the Australian doctors, the British and international cave divers, the Chinese rope-and-pulley specialists, the Japanese irrigation experts, the Thai SEALs, water pump workers, policemen, birds' nest collectors, cooks, barbers, farmers, student swimming-pool volunteers, mapmakers, government officials, and especially Ek and the twelve players, were mastering the cave, the Wild Boars defeated the Northern Kids 5−1. On that day, everybody won. But inside the cave, Ek, four Wild Boars, and three Thai SEALs were still awaiting rescue. And the most treacherous day was yet to come.

Tuesday, July 10: "Landslide!"

Ek, Titan, Mark, Tee, and Pong were still in Chamber Nine, along with three SEALs, Dr. Pak, and Dr. Harris. Bringing out Ek and the four Wild Boars in one day would mean one diver would need to make two trips. Once the team was gone, the SEALs and Dr. Harris would dive themselves out. The divers were getting tired, and the water conditions were worsening.

By now there was zero visibility in the water, which was increasingly littered with debris from the rescue efforts, such as discarded wires and tubes. Swimming in this sludge, a diver could not see craggy rocks until he hit them. Yet making certain that never happened to one of the sleeping boys was crucial. One bang could dislodge the face mask. Now, in the most perilous spots, each diver had to clutch his silent player as close as possible to his face, cheek to cheek through their masks shielding him with his own face and body.

Worse conditions, tired divers, but there were forecasts of new rain, so everyone needed to push on.

One by one, first Ek and then the boys were loaded into skeds, pulled along the guide ropes, carried across the chambers, hoisted along the pulleys, handed from one SEAL to another down the slopes, and brought out of the caverns. Until the first disaster struck.

Fish on came the WhatsApp message in Chamber Three. A diver and a Wild Boar were on the way, tugging the line. So far the rhythm had been the same—message, then tug, then about fifteen minutes later, diver and sleeping young man arrived.

Fifteen minutes went past. No tug.

Thirty minutes.

Forty-five minutes.

Something was wrong. Very wrong.

One hour.

Chris Jewell was the least experienced of the British divers; this was his first cave rescue. In the rapid current between Chambers Four and Three he tried to move his sleeping passenger from one arm to the other while holding the line. His hand slipped and lost the rope. Jewell groped for the line in the black water—not here, not there.

Cave divers know not to panic, not to rush, not to thrash around and worsen the situation. As Brisbin explained, "In that type of true 'zero visibility,' a light does not make any difference in your ability to see through the water. Many divers will simply leave their lights off and work purely by touch."

This is what the experienced cave divers mean about not giving in to panic. You are in extreme danger: you've lost your only guide rope; you're trapped with a sleeping person whose life is your responsibility, in cold water in a cave with absolutely no light—which is the time to think. You assess and arrive at your best, most logical plan. "Emotions," as Hodges said, "are not your friend."

Finally, Jewell's fingers found something solid. Not a line but a sealed electrical cable. No danger of shock, but where would it lead? He trusted that pulling along the cable would take him in the same direction as the rope—to Chamber Three—before the cold water chilled the boy, or the drug wore off.

Jewell guessed, and guessed wrong. He was pulling himself back into the cave, away from the entrance.

Sensing an air pocket, he pulled himself and his sleeping passenger into the waiting cavern. When he looked around, he realized he was back in Chamber Four but nowhere near helpers or the guide rope.

CHAMBER NINE

Mallinson was back on his second journey of the day to bring out the very last Wild Boar: Mark. Mark had the smallest face, making it difficult to find a mask that would completely seal. But Harris had already put Mark to sleep and left on his own journey back. Mallinson tried one mask, then another, then shoved off—hoping this final seal would hold.

CHAMBER FOUR

Speeding along on his return journey, Harris noticed Jewell and his passenger marooned in the cavern. The doctor took the Wild Boar and swam along to Chamber Three.

CHAMBER THREE

Harris emerged, sleeping boy in tow. Sergeant Brisbin rushed to check—"He's alive!" Jewell followed and soon Mallinson, carrying Mark.

Ek, the twelve Wild Boars, and their diver escorts were all out.

That did not mean everyone in the cave was safe.

The people left in Chamber Nine were divers, so the entire "Euro" crew evacuated Chambers Eight through Four and joined the teams in Three. Someone must have assumed that rescuing the team was the only challenge, so the spare oxygen tanks in Three were being taken out. Swimming alone without passengers or the need to go through the medical checkpoints, the last divers would move quickly, so they waited two hours after the last Wild Boar left to begin their swim. They had no support in the cave and no extra tanks left in resupply, but it didn't seem they would need them.

SEAL one arrived in Chamber Three, soon followed by SEAL two.

"LANDSLIDE! LANDSLIDE!"

The code word for immediate disaster rang out in Three. One of the huge pumps that was draining the caves and keeping Chamber Three dry broke (or may possibly have been turned off). Water flooded into the chamber. This was what had happened to the trapped pump workers days earlier—but now there were no extra oxygen tanks left in the chamber. Those who had their own tanks quickly dived out. Those who didn't slid as fast as they could on their bellies across the filling sump. Anderson urgently texted to the few remaining workers, GET OUT, GET OUT; two soldiers sped to the watery sump while raising their heads above the waves to catch any bit of air, their lips nearly scraping the jagged roof. They made it, followed by the SEALs who had been able to dive the treacherous sump using their air. The Chinese were the very last, leaving behind their rope life passage for future visitors to see.

Everyone was accounted for and safe, out of the cave. Ek and the four players were whisked off to the hospital to be checked carefully, to rest, and to be fed. For the moment they had to be out of the spotlight.

10

Rebirth

AFTER THE AMBULANCES SPED AWAY, THE GREEN CURTAIN covering the cave entrance parted. As the waiting crowd clapped and screamed their thanks, exhausted divers in their black wet suits lumbered down the slight incline and through the throng. The Thai SEALs wore sunglasses and green surgical masks—as ever disguising their faces. The rescue was over, and the story was just beginning.

Over the next few days the eager world press would have its moment—rushing to interview every possible participant in words, images, studio recordings, and videotape shot during the mission. Now the competition among nations that had disappeared during the rescue took over. Thai sources told the stories of Thai heroes, while some downplayed or even misreported the stateless status of some of the players. American television filled with the faces of American soldiers. Australian television featured the Australian doctors. British reporters swarmed over their cave divers from the moment their plane landed in London, asked them if they were "heroes"—they said no—and the journalists began talking about knighthood. The Chinese press covered the Chinese team, as the Japanese papers singled out the Japanese irrigation specialist. Canadian TV lingered on the parents of Eric Brown, a Canadian diver who had been a volunteer in the cave. All these stories were true—or, rather, partial truths. Each version told a fraction of a larger tale. A first feature film crew was already on the scene, planning an action-adventure movie with a Christian slant—yet another partial slice of the pie—soon followed by so many other film teams that the Thai Ministry of Culture needed to create a special committee to oversee them all.

The one missing piece, the most important of all, was the voice of the Wild Boars.

Ek and the twelve players were resting in Chiang Rai hospital. Since they had arrived over the course of three days, their recovery was staggered. Each one needed to be carefully checked for infections—a weak person trapped in a closed, humid environment might well have been exposed to bacteria or viruses his body could not fight off. Good news: other than several cases of easily treatable pneumonia, the doctors did not find anything serious. Before parents were even allowed to visit the hospital and to wave at their children through a glass partition, photos were released showing the entire ward with all thirteen seemingly happy, smiling, recovering well. Then the families were brought a step closer—to see their children through the glass window. Titan's father "started to cry, everybody started to cry," he told CNN. "I want to say thanks to those who rescued my boy. And helped him to have a new life; it's like a rebirth."

While parents waited to be told when the Wild Boars would be released, they had a crucial task of their own. Together the boys' parents and close relatives drew a picture of the retired SEAL who had lost his life trying to rescue the team and was now being called "Sergeant Sam." This was not just in memory of him; it was a sacred trust. They all wrote messages of gratitude to Sergeant Sam in Thai and in English and then made the most solemn pledge. If their boys came out of the hospital alive and well, they would all (aside from Adul, since he was not Buddhist) be temporarily ordained as priests—which is not unusual in Thailand. By training in the monastery, they could earn spiritual merit, which they would then donate to Sergeant Sam so that he might have a better rebirth. The families then brought a framed picture with their writing and the shared pledge to the lost sergeant's family.

The ideas of birth and rebirth, and that one person can earn and then pass along merit to another, are central to Buddhism as practiced in Thailand. Parents, for example, often ask a child of theirs—almost always a son—to temporarily enter a monastery as a novice monk to earn merit to give back to the parents. Sergeant Sam had given his life to the boys. The boys, and their families, owed him their commitment and devotion. Speaking from their own belief systems, many of the divers who assisted in the rescue also focused on the loss of Sergeant Sam, and urged people to contribute to a fund set up to assist his wife and children.

Ek and the team were slated to leave the hospital on Thursday,

Ek, to the left with his head down as several of the Wild Boars hold the signed drawing of Sergeant Sam. Titan is in front wearing number 7; behind him is Adul holding one end of the frame, and holding the other end is Tee.

July 19, but they were doing so well, they were going to be released a day early. Thai authorities knew how excited the press would be to hear from the thirteen. All were recovering, but how could they handle the crush of prying questions, the instant fame, the endless requests for interviews? A carefully crafted news conference, with all questions prescreened by mental health professionals so that they would not upset the still-fragile players, was staged on the day Ek and the team were to rejoin their families. And this was a second value of the plan to send the boys to the monastery: once they left the hospital, they would have a bit more time out of the public eye to rest, think, meditate, and heal. As the abbot, or head of the monastery, said, "I hope they will find peace, strength, and wisdom from practicing the Buddha's teaching."

The ninety-minute news conference began by honoring Sergeant Sam. Then, guided by the host, Ek and the team gave the explanations and descriptions of their experiences—from riding their bikes to the cave to spending time with their adopted Thai SEAL "father," Baitei—used in this book. Since Ek and the team had been sedated during the rescue, they had no memory of those dangerous hours—and so that was not discussed. Instead the conference switched to what they had all learned from the experience.

Coach Ek: "I would like to begin by saying that I really appreciate all that everyone has done for our sakes. We will use our lives in a mindful manner; we will be more cautious before acting."

Tee: "I pledge to be a good person for society."

Adul: "From this incident, I've learned that acting without sufficiently thinking can really impact us in not only the short term, but also the long term. With this life that I now have, I will live to the fullest."

Bew: "My dreams have not changed. I still want to become a professional soccer player. However, now I have another dream of becoming a SEAL officer."

Three more team members echoed Bew's feeling—now they, too, wanted to become SEALs. For the moment, though, the boys, other than Adul, said they wanted to enter the monastery and be temporarily ordained as novice priests "in honor of Sergeant Sam."

A Western audience might have wanted to hear more from the players as individuals—what they felt, feared, hoped, learned, experienced—in the cave. There was a strong sense, though, from the boys, their families, and Thai officials, that this was a time for respect, gratitude, healing, and a devotion to service. Interviewed later by a Thai reporter, Sri Tammachoke, the farmer who so willingly gave up her fields, spoke with the same calm, firm, and absolute assurance about the boys' future: "When the boys grow up, they will want to help others in turn. They will be good Thai citizens." This was not a wish—it was a certainty.

A psychologist ended the news conference by speaking to the press, and to the world, urging all to leave the young men alone and let them return to their families, friends, school—their normal lives.

The Thai press listened, but the world's press did not. One TV crew even rushed to Titan's house to capture a few "exclusive" seconds with him on film before the players spent nine days in the monastery performing rituals, avoiding harming any living thing, and training as novice monks. Ek, who had lived in a monastery for ten years earlier in his life, decided to formally become a monk, to make that calling his life.

The Mirror

What does this story have to say to the rest of us? To the Danish diver Ivan Karadzic, the impossible rescue was like a message, as if a force was trying to show us, to tell us something about ourselves. It was, he said, "a mirror." Around the world, even as the rescue was taking place, the issues around nationality, citizenship, and immigration had created deep divisions. The United States government was separating undocumented immigrant parents from their children; other nations were blocking desperate refugees from crossing their borders, treating immigrants with suspicion, defining nationality by religion, bombing their own citizens with poison gas.

In the Royal Cave of the Reclining Woman, people from around the globe, of many faiths or no faith, speaking different languages, worked together—even including military forces that train daily to face one another in combat. Volunteers gave up everything—time, work, family, rice crops—to help in any little or large way they could. Thai SEALs rushed into dangerous terrain they were not trained to handle because twelve boys and their teacher were lost. Adul, the stateless boy, who was not legally a member of any country— the very symbol of the kind of immigrant so many politicians rail against and nations build walls to exclude—Adul, the master of languages, was the one person who was able to speak to the rescuers. He could do so because learning means everything to him, and to other stateless people like him who every day must prove their worth, only to be treated as unworthy. The rescue was a mirror of the best of humanity at a time where leaders trading on fear, on hatred, on the worst of humanity, were whipping up crowds and winning elections.

On July 23, as the boys were settling into the monastery and the press dispersed, a dam being built in nearby Laos broke, killing at least thirty-six people, with hundreds missing and thousands left homeless. The news flickered across screens for a day or two, then disappeared. Laos is in the midst of a massive project to build dams so that it can become the "battery" for the region—selling power to energy-hungry Thailand. The collapse of the dam was not just an immediate tragedy but raised questions about the rush to development—from the poorly built dam to the issue of whether whole river systems really ought to be blocked and diverted. Very few reporters hustled to cover the event or its larger implications.

The entire cave rescue can be, should be, a window into our world. It gives all of us a chance to learn about Thailand, its history, borders, and beliefs. There is so much to discover in the depth and complexity of Thai Buddhist ideas and practices, the generosity of the Thai people, as well as the current tensions around their military government and distant king. The Thai farmer who felt sympathy for her government sees the world so differently from Americans, who are often quick to turn to lawsuits when they think they have been wronged. It is not that one view or the other is "right"; rather, they are different, and it is that variety of world views that the cave rescue invites us to explore.

Ek and the three stateless Wild Boars have been made Thai citizens, and Thailand has promised to work out the larger issue of the stateless by 2024. If the Thai government follows up on that pledge, that could be a model for other countries.

Then there are the many other windows that the cave story opens. Starting in the region, we are alerted to the fate of people and rivers in Laos, and to the Wa, the Shan, and the challenges faced by these ethnic minorities. The Chinese, from volunteers fighting poachers in Zimbabwe to companies building projects across the entire world, are global actors—and even beyond, as their government prepares the 2020 unmanned mission to Mars. We are partners as major global forces—rivals, yes, but also potential collaborators. The more Americans and Chinese are in touch—through visits, study, and shared experiences—the better.

Shifting away from international relations, the volunteer American army has meant that those who do not have family in the military service may know little about it. The military is developing finely tuned managerial skills that allow it to handle crises in challenging environments throughout the world. Too few American civilians know about and appreciate this aspect of military training. Cave diving itself, and the unique training of doctor divers from Australia and cave rescue experts from the United Kingdom, are there to be explored.

All too often we can be mesmerized by our daily and local passions—sports, politics, tweets from friends—while there is a vast, fascinating, changing wider world just beyond us. The cave rescue gave us all a brief glance at that landscape. Come, it seemed to say, explore with me.

On July 25, two days after the dam collapse in Laos, the press announced that a large lake had been found on Mars under the southern polar ice cap. Perhaps there is life there, or we will be able to build a living environment when we reach the red planet. The discovery was like the lowest rung on a ladder inviting us up and out, off our planet. To explore in space requires the kind of training the divers exhibited, the advanced technologies used by the military in the rescue, the clarity and self-control shown by everyone from the Wild Boars to the rescue team. Most of all, though, we need the spirit of international cooperation shown in the cave.

As soon as the British divers found the thirteen and began considering how to rescue them, they emphasized one word and one concept: collaboration. They knew that only the most complete team effort might possibly work. Every other national group and individual shared that understanding. Elon Musk and his engineers were eager to help. But theirs was a solo effort, a tangent to what everyone else was doing together. Aside from the technical questions of whether the sub could have worked, perhaps it is that difference between solo brilliance and team collaboration that finally mattered.

Who knows which person from which land will have the skill, the touch, the intuition we will need in the inhuman conditions beyond this blue planet? We must cultivate the stateless and the privileged, the local volunteer and the international expert. We need one another. A mile and a half deep in a flooded cavern, we showed we have the skills, the tools—mental and physical—to launch out into our solar system and ultimately beyond. Or we can tighten our borders, reject one another, instill hostility in young people, and remain trapped in darkness.

The choice is ours.

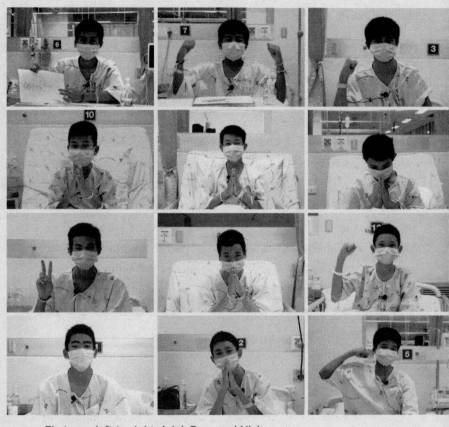

First row, left to right: Adul, Bew, and Nick
Second row, left to right: Titan, Tee, and Dom
Third row, left to right: Night, Pong, and Mark
Fourth row, left to right: Note, Tern, and Mick

How I Researched and Wrote This Book

THE E-MAIL

My family and I were hiking in the Swiss-Italian Alps, guided by Roy Freeman, a childhood friend (his father, Don, created *Corduroy*) who lives in Switzerland and is a professional geologist. He promised my younger son—who loves geography—that he would show us the very spot where the African tectonic plate had smashed into the European tectonic plate millions of years ago. The seven-to-eight-hour days of hiking the steep slopes yielded gorgeous vistas and offered a wonderful break from digital chatter. But at the end of each day, when we reached the so-called hut (built out of stone, it was more like a cross between a barn and a dormitory) where we were staying, there was a weak Wi-Fi signal. As we sat down to dinner one day, I saw a message from an editor I had worked with as a colleague years ago and who was now at Simon & Schuster. She wondered if I would be interested in writing an "instant" book on the just-concluded Thai cave rescue, but she warned me that there would be a very tight schedule.

As we were traveling through Europe I had followed the story, and I had been especially moved by a July 10 article in the *New York Times* titled "Stateless and Poor, Some Boys in Thai Cave Had Already Beaten Long Odds." Just before we left America, my wife, Marina, had organized a reading at our synagogue called Borders of the Heart. Authors read works—their own or those of writers they selected—that explored the experience of being an immigrant. We were reading as our way to speak back to the inhuman immigration policies of our government. Writing can open eyes, open hearts, open borders. The Thai cave story seemed to combine action adventure, drama, and an important story about refugees, immigrants, and crossing borders. And in *Trapped*, my book about the Chilean mine rescue, I had written from limited sources and against a deadline. I wanted to do the Thai book, and since I would not begin teaching until after Labor Day, I thought I could. I e-mailed my agreement to the editor. But I knew I would need help.

RESEARCH

When I worked on *Trapped*, my first step was to find and then print out a full set of news articles from many publications that originally reported on every turn of the drama. Written in the daily press, the articles were limited, and sometimes corrected by later sources, but taken together they gave me the spine of the story. I could then branch out by researching individual actors and themes. I would need a similar library for the Thai book. I teach in the graduate faculty at the Rutgers School of Communication and Information, and I hired two Rutgers doctoral students to help me. Bruce DuBoff is a former head of the New Jersey School Library Association, who has long experience as a middle school librarian. I asked him to research the physical aspects of the cave rescue. Diana Floegel's research interests include issues of youth, gender, and representation, and I asked her to gather information about some of the social and political issues. Dorothy Kelly, a friend and neighbor who wrote her doctoral thesis about several Finnish female artists, became the generalist, helping out in all the searches and helping me compile the proper citations. As I hurried to understand the day-by-day events at the cave, Bruce, Diana, and Dorothy presented me with stacks of neatly marked file folders filled with articles, and they populated a shared Google Doc with further leads.

Reading through the articles, we kept track of names—people I might be able to interview. Bruce, Diana, and Dorothy then used every possible means, from phone, Twitter, and text to e-mail and website, to make contact and ask if I could either send written questions or "meet" the person. Even as we four hunted, read, learned, and sent out queries, I knew I was seeing only a very partial view of the events. Everything we were consulting was in English. Rutgers, of course, has Thai students, but unfortunately, a quirk in our system meant I could not offer to pay them. Dr. Minjie Chen—who is at the Cotsen Children's Library at Princeton—agreed to read the Chinese coverage and then found three wonderful Thai researchers for me. Paradorn ("Joe") Rummaneethorn is a summa cum laude Princeton graduate who has gone on to pursue a doctorate in molecular biology. Tanya Pramongkit is a Thai person living in New York. Nonravee ("Tammy") Benjapibal is a current student at Princeton. With these three strong readers and researchers, I would be able to ask any question about the Thai view of the events and be sure of getting several good answers (which did not mean all would be in agreement). David Jacobson, an author and expert on Japanese children's literature whom I know from our shared involvement in the Global Literature in Libraries Initiative (GLILI), offered to do similar research in Japanese sources. I would not "cover" every language or source, but I was no longer blinded by language.

We began to get responses. Dr. Andrew Alan Johnson, also of Princeton, was an always available, wonderfully informed resource. Divers Ivan Karadzic and Fernando Raigal were generous with their time and began to give me confidence that I could capture the experience of being in the cave. William Stone was a perfect lead into the world of cave diving, told me about Martyn Farr's book, and suggested a way for me to reach Rick Stanton. Getting to interview Rick, who was at the center of the rescue, was thrilling and added a great deal to my knowledge. Rick also responded to several follow-up questions that helped clarify confusions. I contacted Ben Reymenants, who initially agreed to answer my questions, but he later informed me that he is writing his own book and so would not be available.

Major Hodges, Captain Tait, and Staff Sergeant Anderson appeared on many TV programs, but by the time I reached out to them, the military had decided to organize and centralize its presentation of the story. Through Major Savage I was able to attend a teleconference in which he presented a written account of the rescue from the US military point of view, and then Major Hodges and Sergeant Brisbin were available for questions. From what I could tell in the question-and-answer session, I was one of the very few reporters there who was not attached to a military journal, and though I felt a bit out of place, I used my question to learn more about the ROC drill. Major Savage also pointed me to DVIDS, a public website where Captain Tait's photos and raw footage of interviews with Sergeants Galindo and O'Brien were available.

Articles, interviews, and the military resources gave me a lot of information. Through my Thai connections I requested interviews with the SEALs and the Wild Boars but was not able to get a response within my deadline. Governor Osottanakorn, Ek, and Adul came to New York City on October 9, 2018, as part of a world tour and spoke at the Asia Society's Game Changers event. While their appearance was carefully managed and there was no time for extensive questioning, I did have the chance to meet the governor and learn a few more details about the rescue.

The SEALs, Ek, and the team, though, conducted that ninety-minute press conference. The English-language press dipped in for brief highlights. I asked my Thai readers to review it carefully, and Tammy and Joe then supplied me with a complete summary and transcript. Finally, three hour-long TV shows—*Out of the Dark*, created by Australian public television, *Thai Cave Rescue: Against the Elements*, by Thai TV, and "One Way Out: Thailand Cave Rescue" from *20/20* and ABC in America yielded interviews with people I was not able to reach myself.

My job was to assimilate all this material, ask further questions, and then craft the narrative. My best guide was curiosity. Many articles mentioned being "stateless"—but how did that differ from being "undocumented"? Diana sent me a store of articles and even UN documents exploring the issue. When the name Night also appeared as Knight, I realized I needed to understand Thai nick-naming practices. My three Thai researchers and Professor Johnson carefully gave me explanations. When the chronology I managed to cobble together from news sources did not quite make sense, I had to get clarification from Rick—my estimates were off by a day. When I needed to understand the Chinese role better, Dr. Chen passed my questions along to Wang Ke and translated his answers. She also found a long article from the Chinese publication *Outdoor*, which was the most complete description of the cave rescue from Ben Reymenants's point of view. I was question central; my research team then did the great work of helping me find the answers I could weave into this story.

I sent copies of the published book to all of the key actors I could reach. The notes I received back from Stanton and Raigal began a whole new research process. I was now getting direct, primary source information—and learned so much that I had not been able to glean from published reports. I am grateful to Stanton, Raigal, and Christina Soontornvat for pointing out ways that I could improve the original publication.

WRITING

I am immensely fortunate to have a marvelous in-house first reader and editor: my wife, Marina Budhos. Marina pointed out ways to add verve, immediacy, and human drama to the manuscript in general and in many specific sections. My Atheneum editor echoed those notes and made one particularly astute suggestion that significantly helped with the flow of the manuscript. I sent the piece to several divers, my Thai researchers, and Dr. Chen. I heard back from Fernando Raigal late in the process and was pleased that he called it "great work" and that he "actually learned some details that I did not even know." The other divers did not respond in time, and while the comments from the researchers were more general appreciation than specific corrections, I knew at least I was not wrong.

As I was writing the first draft, I aimed to add interest and color by offering brief physical descriptions and character traits of important actors. You can see a remnant of that approach in my descriptions of Master Sergeant Anderson and the farmer Sri Tammachoke. But I was intensely aware that it was easier for me to formulate those descriptions/impressions of Western than of Thai actors. This imbalance was made worse by the fact that outside of one Thai documentary, lengthy video interviews with Western participants were easier to find than parallel views of Thais. I simply saw more of one group than the other. Determined not to fall into the trap of creating a narrative where Western actors are individuals and non-Western actors are a faceless mass of "others," I asked my researchers to help me see key Thai people, starting with Ek and the boys, through Thai eyes. Their responses were fascinating but raised a new set of cultural issues that I thought would complicate rather than enhance the narrative. I decided to remove almost all of those physical-psychological characterizations. Instead, as with Governor Osottanakorn, I focused on how the actions of key Thai personnel have been viewed in Thailand.

RESULTS: ANSWERS AND QUESTIONS

This global quest so soon after the events in the cave produced two important and opposite results. On the one hand, I was amazed to learn several stories that have not been reported in the mainstream press until now. For example, Rick revealed the moment when he and John dove out the four workers, and how it gave them confidence for the later rescue of the boys. Sergeant Brisbin's terrifying wait when the diver and the Wild Boar did not appear at Chamber Three was first revealed in the *20/20* special, but he told more during the question-and-answer portion of the military teleconference and then filled in important details via e-mail. The "Landslide" story was only briefly sketched in the daily press, and the Chinese *Outdoor* article added key details. No one had previously explored the record of the Wild Boars as a soccer team—an avenue of research my older son suggested. On the other hand, there are gaps, contradictions, and questions I was not able to answer. I am certain that books by key participants in the rescue are being written and will shade, revise, or completely correct this account. Here are some of those lingering questions:

I do not fully understand what Tee and Ek did on that first day, when the coach took the rope and descended into the water to try to find the path out of the flooding cave.

I found the ROC drill fascinating and was eager to learn more about it. Unfortunately, the US military did not make any images of it available. The only possible image of it I was able to see was at twenty-nine minutes and twenty-five seconds of the Australian documentary, when they mention the drill and show a very partial photo that might be related.

There is clear tension on both sides between the British divers and the Belgian Ben Reymenants. Key aspects of his account have not stood the test of time. For example, he claimed that the British divers left the cave and that he was given a photo showing they had actually gone to the airport. That is not true. Reymenants said he was the first to reach out to Harris and Challen. He wasn't.

There is no question that Reymenants and Polejaka were the first who crossed the T-junction. After they ran out of rope, the British divers took the lead, found the boys, and were central to the rescue. Both teams of divers played a role in the wonderful outcome. If Reymenants writes his book, he will have more to say from his point of view, as Stanton does in his book *Aquanaut*.

When I first wrote this book, the reasons for bringing Harris and Challen to the cave were not made fully clear. I speculated that the plan to sedate the boys was, in fact, why Stanton had reached out to them. In November 2019, Stanton confirmed that suspicion and told me about an interview with Harris that had just been published. That interview filled in the missing information.

I'd like to know more about how the decision not to use the mini-sub was reached. Though there are reports that Musk himself reached Chamber Three, that has not been corroborated and it seems unlikely. Indeed, Musk's reputation has been significantly undermined by terrible insults he directed at Unsworth, which were totally out of keeping with the spirit of the rescue.

The Thai authorities deliberately obscured which person was being rescued when and by whom. Joe, through very close and careful detective work (during the news conference, the Wild Boars sat in groups based on when they were rescued; he pored over those images, matched faces, and reached his conclusions), arrived at the lineups used in this book. We still don't know who went first, who was the one trapped for an hour when his diver lost touch with the guide rope. We do know that Mark went last, because that was revealed in the *20/20* documentary.

The largest question that later researchers will have to explore has to do with the Thai authorities. The Thais were generous, brave, devoted to the rescue, and extremely receptive to help from other nations. Few if any other people in the world would have been so warm, giving, flexible, and open. Yet the chaos at the cave mouth was a disaster in the making, and there was an undertow hinting at criticisms of the Thai government in some comments from the participants in the rescue.

The military government was popular with some who enjoyed the stability it brought to Thailand, but it has been severely criticized by others for stalling on elections and controlling the press. A government facing both popular criticism and a public relations crisis may well have had difficulty managing the rescue. This strand remains ambiguous because people seemed reluctant to be explicit about judging the role the Thai government played, especially after Sergeant Sam died. Future researchers will need to map the political pressures on the Thai authorities and spell out their decision-making processes. There was a hint of similarly significant caution in how some of the Americans talked about the Chinese presence in the rescue effort. Not any criticism, but rather a certain wariness, which points to ways in which the United States and China are competitors in the region and are very carefully watching each other.

Finally, it would make a wonderful project for a high school or college class to compare the Thai cave rescue story, which drew such consuming attention from the world's media, and the Laos dam tragedy, which did not. Why the disparity? Some answers are obvious: thirteen trapped young people—with the added daily drama of their uncertain fate—make for easier "human interest" pieces than thousands of anonymous displaced families. Thailand is connected to the world's media in ways that Laos is not. While the Thais wanted coverage, the Laotian government is not as eager to host probing reporters. The presence of American, European, and Australian divers and US military drew increased attention from Western media—and provided more English-language interviewees. Still, what is covered in the news—what we see endlessly updated on our screens, what is treated as important and what is not—is a topic we all need to consider.

Notes

PROLOGUE

p. 2: "'Snatch and grab'": Marc Aronson interview with Rick Stanton, August 1, 2018 (hereafter RSI). This story, which is more fully described in chapter 4, does not appear in previous press reports. It had not been public until Rick shared it with me.

CHAPTER 1

p. 3: "'Enthralling'": Andrew Alan Johnson, "Inside the Sacred Danger of Thailand's Caves," The Conversation, July 9, 2018. Downloaded August 5, 2018. theconversation.com/inside-the-sacred-danger-of -thailands-caves-99638.

p. 3: Background on the team comes from the press conference given by the players and Ek on July 18, 2018. Title: ฉบับเต็ม (FULL) แถลง 13หมูป่า เปิดใจครั้งแรก-ส่งหมูป่ากลับบ้าน. Translation (full version): "Disclose 13 Boars First Heart-to-Heart Conversation and Safely Sending Them Home." Video link: youtube.com/watch?time_continue=1&v=DGuy5OoRR4g. Downloaded and translated on August 24, 2018 by Joe (hereafter PC).

p. 5: Figures are also included in Johnson Lai, "Statelessness a Hurdle for Some Boys Rescued From Thai Cave," July 16, 2018. usnews.com/news /world/articles/2018-07-16/statelessness-a-hurdle-for-some-rescued-thai -boys.

p. 5: "players were among the 400,000": Hannah Beech, "Stateless and Poor, Some Boys in Thai Cave Had Already Beaten Long Odds," *The New York Times,* July 10, 2018. Downloaded July 12, 2018. nytimes .com/2018/07/10/world/asia/thailand-cave-soccer-stateless.html.

p. 6: Dr. Johnson explained Thai nicknaming practices in the following e-mail to Marc Aronson on August 14, 2018, used by permission. The note also relates to the nickname Night, which appears in the text on page 8.

Many Thais have nicknames from English. One gets a nickname in order to hide one's true name from any spirits that might be listening. Most people use their nickname as their primary means of address. Many nicknames are English words. Parents might (nick)name their kids "Aey," "Bee," "See" (A, B, C) in order of their birth. Other kids are called Golf, or Benz, or, like my friend, Boy (her parents wanted a boy, you see). So Night versus Knight . . . it's impossible to tell how it should be spelled in Roman characters without asking the kid. In Thai, the name would be pronounced "Nai," anyway—certainly no difference between the two. But my guess is that it's probably an English loanword, although "Nai" is a common Thai name. Depending on the tone, it can mean "duty," "noble," as well as less meaningful things like "inside" or "where?"

Ultimately, nicknames are informal. They're used between friends. One can switch them around and change them. They're rarely written. They're often foreign loanwords. So your task re: getting the "correct" Romanization is, in short, impossible.

p. 6: Titan and his grandmother's stateless status: Matt Blomberg, "In That Cave, Three Thai Boys and Their Coach Had No Escape. Above Ground, They Have No Country," *Los Angeles Times,* July 13, 2018. latimes.com/world/la-fg-thailand-cave-stateless-20180713-story.html.

p. 6: "Titan had been playing soccer": Jacob Goldberg and Veena Thoopkrajae, "Talented and Resilient: The Wild Boars Footballers Trapped in Thai Cave," *The Guardian*, July 5, 2018. This is one of many articles that gave brief descriptions of the players. I used it combined with more details gleaned from the press conference to describe the twelve young men. theguardian.com/world/2018/jul/05/talented-and -resilient-the-wild-boars-footballers-trapped-in-thai-cave.

p. 6: Burma or Myanmar: while Myanmar is the official name and is used in most publications, I chose not to, and this is my reasoning. In the 1960s, as countries became independent and free of their former colonial masters, they quite properly selected new names. For example, Rhodesia, named after the white British colonizer Cecil Rhodes, became Zimbabwe. However, in the late 1970s, the truly genocidal Khmer Rouge took over Cambodia and insisted that the nation be called Kampuchea. Some in the West did so, treating the government as one more liberation movement. The Khmer Rouge were cold-blooded murderers, not liberators. I resisted the change, and, since the horrific crimes of that government have been exposed, the name of the country has reverted to Cambodia. While a nation has every right to name itself, it is worth asking who is speaking in the name of that country and why. The regime that changed Burma's name was a military dictatorship. And while a form of democracy has been restored, the new government has overseen the ethnic cleansing of the Rohingya, a Muslim minority group. It seems fair to me to hold off on accepting the name change of a government that is capable of such acts.

p. 7: "thirteen-year-old Nutchanan Ramkeaw": Warangkana Chomchuen, Phred Dvorak, and Jake Maxwell Watts, "'Where Have You Guys Been?': Thai Cave Challenge Quickly Became a Trap," *The Wall Street Journal*, July 7, 2018. wsj.com/articles/where-have-you-guys-been -thai-boys-cave-challenge-quickly-became-a-trap-1530992411.

p. 7: The observation on how Thai social media were buzzing about Dom and Mark came in an e-mail from Tammy to Marc Aronson, August 15, 2018.

p. 7: Information on the Wa State: Yimou Lee and Antoni Slodkowski, "Myanmar's Remote Wa State Suffers as Fewer Chinese Come to Party," Reuters, January 21, 2017.

p. 8: The many articles on the twelve young men had little to say about Nick. I asked Joe to search in the Thai media, and he discovered the fact that Nick was not actually on the team.

p. 8: "'Since everyone was curious'": PC. Press reports called this event a practice—as if the players were scrimmaging against one another—but in the press conference it was described as an actual game.

p. 9: The legend behind the cave's name is described in Johnson, "Inside the Sacred Danger of Thailand's Caves," cited earlier.

p. 10: "now gushes water—looking, the Belgian diver Ben Reymenants has said, like white water": Radhika Viswanathan, "This Is Madness": A Rescue Diver on What It Was Like to Save the Thai Boys in the Cave," *Vox* (Vox Media website), July 12, 2018. vox.com/2018/7/12/17564360 /thai-cave-rescue-boys-mission-diver-ben-reymenants.

p. 10: "'magnificent'": Dr. Martin Ellis and Shepton Mallet, *The Caves of Northern Thailand* (Somerset, UK: 2017), 151. My thanks to Dr. Chen for finding this guide, which also mentions that the author, along with Vern Unsworth and Rob Harper, had explored the cave.

p. 13: "'When you're in the cave'": Michael Safi and Veena Thoopkrajae, "Left Behind: The Two Thai Boys Who Missed Out on Disastrous Cave Trip," *The Guardian*, US Edition, July 5, 2018. Downloaded August 2, 2018. theguardian.com/world/2018/jul/05 /thai-soccer-boys-missed-cave-trip-wild-boars. Many press reports claimed that the Wild Boars could not swim. The team explicitly corrected that impression during the press conference.

p. 13: "Reassured," "'running out of breath'": PC.

p. 13: Account of Ek's dive, Fernando Raigal to MA, October 19, 2019.

p. 14: "'Do you know where Ek is?'": Safi and Thoopkrajae, "Left Behind," cited earlier.

p. 14: Information about the local rescue team came from the Thai documentary *Thai Cave Rescue: Against the Elements*, hereafter TCR.

p. 15: "'Ek! Ek! Ek!'" Shabani Mahtani, "'He Loved Them More Than Himself': How a 25-Year-Old Former Monk Kept the Thai Soccer Team Alive," *The Washington Post*, July 7, 2018. Downloaded July 18, 2018. washingtonpost.com/world/asia_pacific/he-loved-them-more -than-himself-how-a-25-year-old-former-monk-kept-the-thai-soccer-team -alive/2018/07/07/b4100076-815e-11e8-b3b5-b61896f90919_story .html?utm_term=.c7b8cc722b9b.

CHAPTER 2

p. 16: Tammy provided me with a summary of Thai views of the governor in an e-mail of September 19, 2018. Here is a link to an article in Thai she used as one resource: thestandard.co/chiang-rai-governor -narongsak-osot-thanakorn.

p. 16: "'No one really had any idea'": BBC, "The Full Story of Thailand's Extraordinary Cave Rescue," July 14, 2018. Downloaded July 18, 2018. bbc.com/news/world-asia-44791998.

p. 17: History of the SEALs, navyseals.com/nsw/navy-seal-history. Downloaded July 20, 2018. I watched this PBS documentary about the SEALs on July 10, 2018: pbs.org/about/blogs/news/new-pbs-documentary- reveals-the-untold-story-of-the-us-navy-seals. Information about the SEALs and atomic bombs can be found here: smithsonianmag.com/smart-news/25- years-us-special-forces-carried-miniature-nukes-their-backs-180949700.

p. 18: The history of SEALs in Thailand was researched by Tammy, sent to me on July 20, 2018, and was based on these links: sealthailand.com /index1.htm, and tnews.co.th/contents/193647.

p. 18: "'Men with green faces'" and their missions are described in the PBS documentary.

p. 19: "'It makes me realize'" and information on Thailand's king: Richard C. Paddock and Ryn Jirenuwat, "As Search for Thai Boys Lost in Cave Hits Day 5, a Nation Holds Its Breath," *The New York Times*, June 27, 2018. Downloaded August 1, 2018. nytimes.com/2018/06/27/world/asia/thailand-cave-soccer-search.html.

p. 20: "'Scuba diving is a sport, a hobby'" and subsequent quotations from Ivan Karadzic: Marc Aronson interview, July 23, 2018.

p. 20: "'With cave diving,'" Rick Stanton interview, Divernet 10/2007. Downloaded July 23, 2018. archive.divernet.com/cave-diving/p302428-rick-stanton.html.

p. 20: William Stone interview with Marc Aronson, August 3, 2018.

p. 22: "'We wanted to be'": "The Full Story of Thailand's Extraordinary Cave Rescue" (no author cited), BBC.com, July 14, 2018. Downloaded July 18, 2018. bbc.com/news/world-asia-44791998.

p. 22: "Like everyone in Thailand": Chomchuen, Dvorak, and Watts, "'Where Have You Guys Been?'"

p. 22: For the arrival of the singer and her assistant's brother: Phred Dvorak and Jake Maxwell Watts, "The Thai Cave Rescue, Before Its Triumph, Teetered on the Brink of Disaster," *The Wall Street Journal*, July 11, 2018.

p. 23: For Sophia Thaianant: See Susan Muthalaly, "Meet the Muslim Team Who Helped to Feed the Thai Cave Rescue Mission," My Salaam, July 11, 2018. Downloaded August 8, 2018.

CHAPTER 3

p. 25: "'As you enter'": Marc Aronson interview with Fernando Raigal, July 22, 2018.

p. 26: Information on Captain Surawan from TCR.

p. 27: "'We went in a few kilometers'": Associated Press, "Flood Waters Hamper Efforts to Rescue Boys Missing in Thai Cave," *The*

Guardian, June 25, 2018. Downloaded August 2, 2018. theguardian.com /world/2018/jun/25/thailand-cave-search-boys-missing-chiang-rai -province.

p. 28: "'If they're in the right place'"; "'Divers are in dark areas'": Hannah Ellis-Peterson, "Cave Boys' Relatives Keep Vigil as Rescue Effort Grips Thailand," *The Guardian,* June 29, 2018. Downloaded August 2, 2018. theguardian.com/world/2018/jun/29/cave-boys-relatives-keep-vigil-as-rescue-effort-grips-thailand.

pp. 29–30: Information on Wang Ke supplied by Dr. Chen, based on this Chinese newspaper article, bjwb.bjd.com.cn/html/2018-07/19/content_266286.htm (downloaded August 8, 2018) and questions of mine she passed along to him in an interview conducted on my behalf (August 18, 2018) and his response and additional comments (September 25, 2018).

Dr. Chen sent these links to articles in Chinese and English about both of the Chinese teams who came to Thailand on August 5, 2018: [English] chinadaily.com.cn/a/201807/05/WS5b3d537fa3103349141e0c0b.html.

[English] jqknews.com/news/37638-The_missing_football_team_in_Thailand_was_found_Thai_Prime_Minister_thanked_rescue_workers.html.

[Chinese] thepaper.cn/newsDetail_forward_2257968.

[Chinese] infzm.com/content/137381.

p. 32: "Ek felt responsible for putting the team in danger": Beech, "Stateless and Poor."

p. 32: Information on the Shan, e-mail from Dr. Johnson, August 6, 2018.

pp. 32–33: Ek's family background ("By the time Ek was ten, both of his parents and his brother had died. After two years of being . . ."): Sutton, "How a 25-Year-Old Former Monk."

p. 33: Description of meditation: Andrew Alan Johnson, "The Rescued Thai Boys Are Considering Becoming Monks—Here's Why," The

Conversation (no date). Downloaded August 5, 2018. theconversation
.com/the-rescued-thai-boys-are-considering-becoming-monks-heres-why
-99992; and Marc Aronson interview with Dr. Johnson July 19, 2018.

p. 33: On meditation, "Western scientists have": No author cited, "How
Meditation Helped Trapped Thai Boys Stay Calm," *Newport Academy*, July
11, 2018. Downloaded July 18, 2018. newportacademy.com/resources
/empowering-teens/mindfulness-for-teens.

Brigid Schulte, "Harvard Neuroscientist: Meditation Not Only
Reduces Stress, Here's How It Changes Your Brain," *The Washington Post*,
May 26, 2015. Downloaded July 18, 2018. washingtonpost.com/news/
inspired-life/wp/2015/05/26/harvard-neuroscientist-meditation-not-
only-reduces-stress-it-literally-changes-your-brain/?utm_term
=.5284e33ca2e9.

p. 33: "According to his aunt, Ek would spend": Tassanee Vejpongsa
and Grant Peck, "Buddhist Meditation May Calm Team Trapped in
Thai Cave," AP News, July 6, 2018. Downloaded July 18, 2018. apnews
.com/18bb8b28150a47d5a647976a0642a3f1.

p. 34: All descriptions of the team in the cave are from PC. Some news
articles reported that the team did bring some food into the cave with
them and that Ek gave up his portion to feed the boys. In the press
conference, they stressed that they did not have any food at all.

CHAPTER 4

p. 35: "'There is a soccer'": Major Charles Hodges quoting the message
he received. I saw this in the Australian one-hour special *Out of the Dark*,
produced by Channel 4, Australian public television; further descriptions
from the account of the mission written by Major Savage and e-mailed to
me on August 8, 2018 (hereafter Mil).

p. 36: Brisbin story, Mil.

p. 37: "Chris Jewell and Jason Mallinson . . . most skilled, fearless cave
divers in the world": Roland Oliphant and Helena Horton, "Meet the
Seven British Divers Playing Leading Roles in the Thai Cave Rescue

Mission," *Telegraph,* July 11, 2018. telegraph.co.uk/news/2018/07/09 /meet-seven-british-divers-playing-leading-roles-thai-cave-rescue.

p. 38: "'They are like'": Martyn Farr, *The Darkness Beckons* [hereafter DB] (Sheffield, UK: Vertebrate Publishing, 2017), 224; "a strong survival," 234.

p. 38: "'Stanton first heard about cave diving'": Brendon O'Brian, "Rick Stanton," *Diver,* October 2007. Downloaded from Divernet July 31, 2018. archive.divernet.com/cave-diving/p302428-rick-stanton.html.

p. 38: "'If you are lucky,'" RS.

p. 39: Florida deaths, DB, 264; survey, L. Polts et al., "Thirty Years of American Cave Diving Fatalities," Pubmed, ncbi.nlm.nih.gov/pubmed /27723015.

p. 39: "'You're in an environment'": Matt Rudd, "Interview: John Volanthen, British Diver Behind the Thai Cave Rescue Attempt," *Sunday Times,* July 8, 2018. thetimes.co.uk/article/british-rescuer-s-survival -guide-do-it-right-never-panic-k7hhvvwhc.

p. 40: "'Even imagine,'" from *Out of the Dark.*

p. 41: "'Undiveable'": Laura Seligman, "Mission Impossible: Inside the Dramatic Cave Rescue of a Thai Soccer Team," Foreign Policy September 20, 2018. Downloaded September 20, 2018. My thanks to Doni Remba for bringing this article to my attention. foreignpolicy.com/2018/09/20/ mission-impossible-inside-the-dramatic-cave-rescue-of-a-thai-soccer-team.

p. 41: "Flown from . . . to the site by AirAsia": Matt Pond, "Cave Man: Phuket Diver Ben Reymenants Relives Four Days in Tham Luang Cave Rescue Mission," *Phuket News,* July 7, 2018. thephuketnews.com/cave -man-phuket-diver-ben-reymenants-relives-four-days-in-tham-luang-cave -rescue-mission-67785.php#R4ZuB07WjwCJqgBm.97.

p. 41: Water conditions in the cave, MA conversation with RS, November 4, 2019.

p. 42: Information on Srivara Rangsibrahmanakul came to me in an e-mail from Tammy on September 19, 2018.

p. 43: This more extended version of the story outlined in the prologue comes from RS.

CHAPTER 5

pp. 46–47: "'This is madness,'" "'These boys,'" "'I can't face'": Viswanathan, "This Is Madness."

p. 47: "'Massive cavern'": Footage of interview with Galindo, dvidshub .net/video/619036/thai-rescue-interview. This site is accessible by the public, but you must request and obtain permission before you can view the material on it. Downloaded August 10, 2018.

p. 48: "'Everyone,' Governor Osottanakorn admitted, 'is discouraged'": TCR

p. 48: "'I was shocked and crying'": Thai coverage, translated by Joe: youtube.com/watch?v=tE83VdsZN7I (published June 25, 2018). "Parents confident their children will survive, trust the coach won't abandon them since he has brought them here many times before."

p. 48: "General Prayut Chan-o-cha . . . arrived to support and encourage": Hannah Ellis-Peterson, "Cave Boys' Relatives Keep Vigil as Rescue Effort Grips Thailand," *The Guardian,* June 29, 2018. Downloaded August 2, 2018. theguardian.com/world/2018/jun/29/cave-boys -relatives-keep-vigil-as-rescue-effort-grips-thailand.

p. 48: Characterization of the governor: e-mail from Tammy summarizing Thai coverage, September 19, 2018.

p. 49: "people from all over Thailand and across the globe": Pam Mengqi, "Dedicated Team Members Quick to Spring into Action in Thailand," *China Daily,* July 5, 2018. Downloaded August 2, 2018. usa .chinadaily.com.cn/a/201807/05/WS5b3d537fa3103349141e0c0b.html.

p. 51: Information on the chores Ek assigned and the sense of brotherhood, PC.

p. 51: "Far away in Chile, Omar Reygadas": Eva Vergara, "Chilean

Miner Offers Advice to Trapped Thai Soccer Team," AP News, July 3, 2018. apnews.com/80e4b79018f143e4bad5125b92631882.

p. 52: Benavides, "'It's valuable for them'": Darran Simon and Taylor Barnes, "Lessons from Chile: Two Doctors Involved in the Rescue of 33 Trapped Chilean Miners Share Their Insight," CNN.com, July 4, 2018. cnn.com/2018/07/04/asia/chilean-doctors-miners-rescue-thailand -cave-intl/index.html.

p. 52: Description of farmer and "'if the water'": TCR. Getting to see some Thai perspectives not covered at all in the Western press was a real treat this documentary offered.

p. 53: Galindo described this journey in his DVIDS interview.

p. 54: "'We had to dive'": Chomchuen, Dvorak, and Watts, "'Where Have You Guys Been?'"

CHAPTER 6

pp. 55–56: "On Sunday three": MA conversation with RS, November 4, 2019.

p. 56: Story of Chinese team and the false rumor: Dong Jun, Song Mingwei, and Gao Bin, "Out of the Abyss," *Outdoor* [hereafter *Outdoor*], provided by Dr. Chen with Google Translate version in English on September 24, 2018. She then reviewed the somewhat garbled text with me.

pp. 56-58: "Leading off the": MA conversation with RS, November 4, 2019, and further e-mails from RS to MA, November 5, 2018–June 19, 2019.

p. 58: "'Trophy,'" Stone interview.

p. 58: "Images," RS.

p. 59: A rumor among some divers: In an interview with Garry Holden of the Thaiger Reymenants says that the team was not at Pattaya Beach but farther in the cave, and then says the Thai authorities wanted a Thai medic to be the first to reach them. Ben Reymenants's interview with

Garry Holden. The Thaiger 102.75 FM. youtube.com/watch?v=YIP -19OB588.

pp. 61–62: I watched many versions of the video and transcribed the words. I asked Terry to add additional translations of the Thai discussions among the boys, which were not translated in English-language sources.

p. 62: Worry about getting the boys out, RS.

p. 62: It is possible that the SEALs who swam back from Chamber Nine were able to add to their supply of gas by taking tanks not needed by those who remained with the boys, but I have not been able to confirm that.

CHAPTER 7

p. 66: "First thought": *Out of the Dark*, cited earlier.

p. 67: "'It's important'": article in Japanese translated by David Jacobson and e-mailed to me August 14, 2018. weibo.com/ttarticle/p/ show?id=2309404272600292451530.

p. 67: Information on the Thai geologist from OCR.

p. 67: "While pumps could": MA conversation with RS, November 4, 2019.

pp. 67-68: Harris and Challen information from *Out of the Dark*.

p. 67: "In Australia two": MA conversation with RS, November 4, 2019.

p. 68: Mallinson excerpt from *Out of the Dark*.

p. 69: "'Once I'": Lauren Ferri, "'We Pulled It Off': Australian Divers Who Played a Key Role in Saving 12 Kids from a Flooded Thai Cave in a Famous Rescue Tell the Full Story of Their Mission for the First Time—and Reveal They Were Convinced the Boys Would All Die." Daily Mail. November 3, 2019 (updated November 4, 2019). dailymail .co.uk/news/article/=7644313/Australian-doctors-saved-12-soccer -players-coach-flooded-Thai-cave-tell-story.html (accessed November 5, 2019).

p. 69: Musk story: Li Zhou, "Elon Musk and the Thai Cave Rescue: A Tale of Good Intentions and Bad Tweets," *Vox*, July 18, 2018. vox .com/2018/7/18/17576302/elon-musk-thai-cave-rescue-submarine.

p. 69: "Like family" and all details of the SEALs, Ek, and the boys in the cave: PC.

p. 71: Theories on Gunan's death, Fernando Raigal to MA, October 9, 2019.

p. 71: Interview with Gunan's wife and the governor's characterization: news.com.au/lifestyle/real-life/news-life/saman-gunan-tragedy-you-are -the-hero-in-my-heart/news-story/fef684306c15114ced519feb862fe261. Downloaded August 26, 2018.

p. 71: The motto of the pararescue team is described and discussed in the Galindo and O'Brien DVIDS interviews.

p. 72: Information on oxygen deprivation: water-for-health.co.uk/ our-blog/2016/11/symptoms-oxygen-deficiency-yes-real-health-issue. Downloaded August 26, 2018.

p. 72: "Musk had sent his engineers": Li Zhou, "Elon Musk and the Thai Cave Rescue."

p. 73: Anderson, "We either have a shot" and Hodges: Gutman et al., "Thai Cave Rescuers."

p. 73: Versions of this moment also appear in Mil and *Out of the Dark*.

CHAPTER 8

p. 75: "Chinese . . . felt welcomed," "'they took care of our emotions'": Chen Yi, "Experience the Cave Rescue in the Eyes of the Chinese Team Members for Eighteen Days," infzm.com, July 12, 2018. infzm.com/ content/137381. (You will need an account in order to read this article.) Dr. Chen supplied this link, which I read through Google Translate: infzm.com/content/137381.

pp. 75–76: "They could rely": MA conversation with RS, November 4, 2019.

pp. 75–76: How the map was created: Brett Dixon, "The Technology Behind the Cave Rescue," Esri Blog, July 18, 2018. esri.com/about /newsroom/blog/technology-behind-thailand-cave-rescue.

p. 78: An Israeli company claimed that it had supplied a communication system that did work in the cave, but the Americans stressed the use of only Vietnam-era walkie-talkies and WhatsApp. This is a detail someone will have to work out. See Max Schindler, "Israeli Technology to the Rescue for Cave-Trapped Thai Boys," *Jerusalem Post*, July 6, 2018. jpost.com/Israel -News/Israeli-technology-to-the-rescue-for-cave-trapped-Thai-boys-561806.

pp. 79–80: This outline of the forces and chambers came from Mil.

p. 80: ROC described in Mil.

p. 81: The school rehearsal is described in several sources including Mil and *Out of the Dark*.

p. 81: "Ruengrit Changkwanyuen": Dvorak and Watts, "The Thai Cave Rescue, Before Its Triumph."

p. 82: "'Tiny kid-sized'": Li Zhou, "Elon Musk and the Thai Cave Rescue."

p. 82: "'I can't have'": ABC/*20/20* documentary, "One Way Out: Thailand Cave Rescue."

p. 84: "'I could only worry,'" PC.

pp. 84–85: Notes from kids: Liam Cochrane and Supattra Vimonsuknopprat, "Thai Cave Rescue: Boys Write to Their Parents with Love, Food Requests and 'Don't Forget My Birthday,'" ABC News, July 8, 2018. abc.net.au/news/2018-07-07/thai-cave-rescue-boys-write-to-their-parents-with-love2c-food/9953510.

For the notes, see Rebecca Wright and Angie Puranasamriddhi, "Boys, Soccer Coach Trapped in Thai Cave Exchange Notes with Families," CNN, July 11, 2018.

p. 86: The idea that people should leave based on where they lived was discussed in PC.

CHAPTER 9

p. 89: The details of the sedative were explained in "One Way Out."

p. 89: Additional details from Lauren Ferri, "'We Pulled It Off': Australian Divers Who Played a Key Role in Saving 12 Kids from a Flooded Thai Cave in a Famous Rescue Tell the Full Story of Their Mission for the First Time—and Reveal They Were Convinced the Boys Would All Die." Daily Mail. November 3, 2019 (updated November 4, 2019). dailymail.co.uk/news/article/=7644313/Australian-doctors-saved-12-soccer-players-coach-flooded-Thai-cave-tell-story.html (accessed November 5, 2019).

p. 90: Mallinson discusses the oxygen mixture in "One Way Out" and *Out of the Dark.*

p. 90: "The drug was wearing off": Gutman et al., "Thai Cave Rescuers."

p. 90: The boy waking story is described in "One Way Out."

p. 90: Harris's calculations of ketamine doses: MA conversation with RS, November 4, 2019.

p. 91: Brisbin's account is from Mil.

p. 92: "'Learn the rocks'": FR interview with Marc Aronson.

p. 93: Harris's assumption that four of he boys were dead: Lauren Ferri, "'We Pulled It Off': Australian Divers Who Played a Key Role in Saving 12 Kids from a Flooded Thai Cave in a Famous Rescue Tell the Full Story of Their Mission for the First Time—and Reveal They Were Convinced the Boys Would All Die." Daily Mail. November 3, 2019 (updated November 4, 2019). dailymail.co.uk/news/article/=7644313/Australian-doctors-saved-12-soccer-players-coach-flooded-Thai-cave-tell-story.html (accessed November 5, 2019).

p. 93: "'Hotwash,'" Mil.

p. 94: Joe worked out the groupings of Wild Boars for each of the days by very carefully studying their faces and seating at the press conference, where they were grouped by the day they were rescued.

p. 94: "Musk himself": Li Zhou, "Elon Musk and the Thai Cave Rescue."

p. 95: Joe found the story of the July 9 regional soccer game here: [Thai] m.facebook.com/story.php?story_fbid=10158068266139848& id=131732549847&_rdrvoicetv.co.th/read/Sks0HJ-XQ. (You will need a Facebook account to view this video.)

pp. 95–96: The landslide story was explained in Mil and further elaborated from the Chinese point of view in the *Outdoor* article.

p. 98: Brisbin told the story of waiting in the Q and A after the end of the military teleconference on August 8, 2018; the story was further elaborated by Chris Jewell in "One Way Out."

CHAPTER 10

pp. 100–101: "British reporters swarmed": "Thailand Cave Rescue Brit Diver Says, 'We are Not Heroes,'" *BBC News*, July 12, 2018. bbc.com /news/uk-england-bristol-44805343.

p. 101: "So many other film teams": Joe Berkowitz, "The Amount of Thai Cave Rescue Movies in the Works Is Ridiculous," *Fast Company*, July 20, 2018. fastcompany.com/90205733/the-amount-of-thai-cave-rescue -movies-in-the-works-is-ridiculous.

p. 101: "Titan's father": Euan McKirdy, James Griffiths, Steve George, "Tears as Thai Boys See Parents for the First Time Since Cave Rescue," CNN, July 11, 2018. cnn.com/2018/07/11/asia/thai-cave-rescue -aftermath-intl/index.html.

pp. 103–104: "Head of the monastery": Shehab Khan, "Thai Cave Boys Ordained as Monks and Novices as They Stay in Monastery for Nine Days," *Independent*, July 24, 2018. independent.co.uk/news/world/asia /thai-cave-boys-monks-novices-monastery-rescue-football-team -a8461791.html.

p. 104: Dr. Johnson explained some aspects of Thai beliefs about earning and granting merit in "The Rescued Thai Boys Are Considering Becoming Monks—Here's Why"; and Marc Aronson interview with Dr. Johnson, July 19, 2018.

p. 104: Quotations are from PC.

p. 105: "Interviewed later by a Thai reporter": OCR.

p. 105: "'A mirror'": IK interview with Marc Aronson, July 23, 2018.

p. 106: "Laos is in the midst": Mike Ives, "Laos Dam Failure Exposes Cracks in a Secretive Government's Agenda," *The New York Times*, July 29, 2018. nytimes.com/2018/07/29/world/asia/laos-dam-response -government.html.

p. 108: Large lake on Mars: Kenneth Chang and Dennis Overbye, "A Large Body of Water on Mars is Detected, Raising the Potential for Alien Life," *New York Times*, July 25, 2018. nytimes.com/2018/07/25/science /mars-liquid-alien-life.html.

For Further Reading and Viewing

As of this writing, there are no books about the Thai cave rescue, though surely there will be, as well as a number of films, perhaps both reenactments and documentaries. For anyone who would like to learn more, here are some suggestions.

NEWSPAPERS

The New York Times, *The Guardian* (from the UK), *The Straits Times* (Singapore) and many other publications around the world followed the story as it developed and then published summary pieces at the end. There, they pulled together a coherent narrative, often with many images and diagrams. I suggest beginning with these three, as they are in English but from different lands, and also because some papers made use of services such as Associated Press, which means that you might see the same article in several places. The three papers listed here did their own reporting. I found articles from *The Wall Street Journal* and the BBC (UK television) also to be particularly useful. Compile different versions, compare and contrast them, and you will begin to develop your own list of key actors, your own questions left unanswered, your own picture of what took place.

VIDEO

The three TV documentaries—*Out of the Dark*, created by Australian public television, *Thai Cave Rescue: Against the Elements*, by Thai TV (English subtitles), and "One Way Out: Thailand Cave Rescue" from *20/20* and ABC—are well worth viewing to extend and enhance the newspaper reporting. See also the *New York Times* video, *Thai Cave Rescue: How Divers Pulled It Off*.

BACKGROUND

All these sources recount the story of the rescue. To move past the daily events to a deeper understanding of the moment, I suggest exploring the beliefs and practices of Theravada Buddhism, which is the faith of 94 percent of the people in Thailand, getting a sense of the history, geography, and culture of northern Thailand, and looking into the recent political tensions in Thailand. Beliefs, place, and politics help put everyone's actions into their own context. I had some knowledge of all three before I began and used basic Internet searches to fill in details. For someone starting without that initial foundation, I always suggest beginning with a book—which has a named author and should have clear source citations—and then turning to the Internet for more specifics and recent information.

There are many sources on US Navy SEALs, ranging from the kind of overview history available from the SEALs themselves on their website, navyseals.com, to the PBS documentary *Navy SEALs: Their Untold Story*. It is important to recognize that all of these are strongly supportive of the SEALs and that some missions they have been asked to perform have been criticized, even by retired SEALs. I am not aware of as many resources on pararescue teams. That would be an excellent subject to research.

Martyn Farr's book *The Darkness Beckons* is a beautifully illustrated introduction to the history—triumphant and tragic—of cave diving. It does, though, assume a basic interest in and understanding of cave diving and its terminology.

How to Write Research Papers:
A Research Guide Using Marc Aronson's *Trapped* and *Rising Water*

BOOK SUMMARIES

Trapped: How the World Rescued 33 Miners from 2,000 Feet Below the Chilean Desert is the true story of the thirty-three miners trapped in a Chilean mine for more than two months. Based on interviews, news reports, and other research, Aronson uses a dual narrative of "Above" and "Below" to describe the tension and high emotions surrounding both the survival of the miners and the rescue effort to save them. Photos of the mine site, maps of the San José Mine, and illustrations of the massive equipment used in the rescue effort greatly enhance this true story of desperation and triumph.

Rising Water: The Story of the Thai Cave Rescue is the true story of the Wild Boars, a Thai soccer team that got lost in Tham Luang cave and captured the attention of the world. *Rising Water* describes the international rescue operation in which cave-diving experts from all over the world collaborated on this delicate mission, factoring in concern for their own safety and for that of the trapped soccer team and coach. The boys needed to be rescued underwater, but how?

WRITING A RESEARCH GUIDE

You've been assigned to create a book-based research project. Your goal is not to write a summary of the book, but an actual report on an original topic related to the book. Using issues related to *Rising Water* and *Trapped*, this guide will lead you through the process for any research topic.

When thinking of good research techniques, remember QVC: Quality, Vetting, Compatibility.

Quality: use high-quality resources. You may already have print resources; however, don't assume that books and magazines are your only tools for proper research. The Internet can also provide some good, authoritative reference material, if you know where to look. One way to do this safely is with a WebQuest provided by your teacher or librarian.

Vetting: Some of you will likely Google for answers regardless of your teachers' suggestions, and that's allowed, but make sure you evaluate the information you find. One way of evaluating, or vetting, your findings is to seek out information about the website, which you can include in your paper as part of your bibliography. Provide information on the creator or owner of the website, the author of the article or information you read, the date it was created, the name of the page, and, most importantly, your rationale for using this website and accepting it as valid. (You can usually find the creator of the website on the About tab, often located at the very bottom of the web page.) Where did the author get the information? If it is outdated or from sources that do not seem credible, that should affect your decision to use it.

Compatibility: Targeted searches are the easiest way to find research compatible with your chosen topic. The most powerful online searching tool is the use of quotation marks. Consider the following searches* based on *Rising Water*:

- thai cave rescue—4,790,000 hits
- "thai cave rescue"—1,360,000 hits
- "thai cave rescue" map and timeline—92,500 hits
- "thai cave rescue map" and timeline—538 hits

Google Chrome downloads as of 2/14/19

Note how using quotation marks reduced the hits from 4,790,000 to 538.

Dr. Aronson had to approach *Trapped* and *Rising Water* like a student researcher: He brainstormed, exploring topics surrounding mine disasters and cave diving rescues, searching for significant aspects and people to decide what was important, relevant, and most interesting to his audience; those decisions became the books.

You, too, can investigate information about the Thailand cave situation in a similar manner by accessing news websites as well as sites that discuss more specific topics, like the potential for an event to cause post-traumatic stress disorder (PTSD).

RESEARCH PROCESS

In both *Trapped* and *Rising Water*, Dr. Aronson describes his research process, and maps out how he quickly compiled and organized the disparate topics and massive amount of information needed for the books. In the notes and bibliography sections, he also tells readers where he found all his information. These tools can be used as models for a basic, annotated search process. Dr. Aronson used the following steps once he had his topics:

- brainstormed format and method
- outlined what he thought he needed in detail
- procured multimedia data, some of which worked its way into the final book and some of which did not. (It's perfectly fine not to include all data in the final product; it is always better to collect more than you will use.)
- organized the data into connected sections
- separated the useful data from the irrelevant data
- wrote and rewrote based on outlines that he had been revising and expanding during the entirety of both, since things will change during research

The research process described above is the model for the Information Search Process chart. This model is based on Kuhlthau's 1991 Information Search Process: wp.comminfo.rutgers.edu/ckuhlthau/information-search-process.

SIX ACTIVITIES TO HELP WRITE YOUR RESEARCH PAPER

1. **Initiation**: Brainstorm topics and consider some of the specific issues involved with these topics. Start thinking about what topics and issues sound most interesting to you, and list them.

2. **Selection of a topic**: Once you have created your list of topics and issues, you can narrow down your selection by asking questions of interest using the five *W*s (Who, What, Where, When, Why). For example, if copper, drilling, or diving are topics of interest, you may ask questions like: Why is copper so important that people are willing to risk death to mine it? How much does a gigantic drill like the Strata 950 cost? What is it made of? How are the dangers of cave diving similar to those for all types of diving? How are they different? Hopefully, asking yourself these kinds of questions will result in a researchable topic of interest.

3. **Explore the topic**: This is a good time to hit the encyclopedias, books, magazines, and online databases to build a background in your topics. Learn the lingo, understand the important concepts, and develop the questions you want to answer. This is your project, so you have freedom of choice. Decide if this is the topic for you; if you want to change it, now is the time.

4. **Formulate the topic**: This is a perfect time for outlining, either formal or bulleted. Start by creating a logical timeline or progression of points for your paper. You can begin with a list of questions and then answer them through your research. Your outline is your list. Outlining is another self-reflective activity that gets you to question your topics and to begin to see sense in your arguments. For instance, you may learn that copper is essential in

electronics, discover that cave diving is a popular activity, or realize that poorly maintained mines are connected to socioeconomic conditions near the mines, etc.

5. **Collect the data**: Once you have decided on a topic and outlined it, it is time to collect the information that will be used in the research paper. When determining what the best sources are, remember to require justifications, as described earlier, for using that particular source over a database or print item. Reasons will often include timeliness of the data. Remember that lots of data provides lots of choices; limited data provides limited choices. At this point, more is more; during editing, less will be more.

6. **Present the data/Write the paper**: This is the time to write a thesis statement and a research paragraph. Once you know how to do that, all you will need is an introduction and a conclusion.

A thesis statement is the engine of the paper and should be either the first or last sentence of the introduction. It provides significance and power to all the points being made within. It usually provides a setting or context to the issue and a brief statement of the problem within that issue. For example, "In Chilean mining, the 2010 accident caused repercussions in the mining industry that are still felt today" or "The Thai cave rescue operation of 2018 demonstrated the extreme dangers of cave diving."

Think of a research paragraph like a sandwich. The top bun is the introduction of the data—where you establish the data, place it in context, and/or prepare the reader for it. The middle is the meat, the data itself; it can be raw, like cheese (primary citation), or cooked by the author, like a hamburger (secondary citation). The bottom bun is the explanation of why the data is significant; what makes it align with the thesis statement, what makes it indispensable to your paper. Try not to write extremely long paragraphs; you are better off making one or two points well than four points poorly. Once you have your research paragraph, introduction, and conclusion, then you are ready to rock. Good luck!

Adapted from a guide written by Bruce DuBoff, who spent twenty-five years in education, mostly as a middle-school librarian; he is also a past president of the New Jersey Association of School Librarians. Bruce works with Dr. Aronson at Rutgers University, where he is earning his PhD in Library and Information Science. He worked for Dr. Aronson on the research for Rising Water.

Acknowledgments

My thanks to Erin Cox, my agent, for guiding this speedy project along; to my sons, Sasha and Rafi, for putting up with a dad who disappeared into his office for a month; to Marina for everything; to my editor, Reka Simonsen, and her helpful assistant, Julia McCarthy; to my Rutgers colleagues and students who have given me an academic home; and to the brilliant group of researchers who scoured the world's publications to make this book possible. I loved immersing myself in this work of research and writing. I owe a special debt of gratitude to editors at Candlewick and Chronicle, who graciously indulged me in missing their deadlines to allow this project to zoom ahead.

While working on this truly international project I was sustained by many local friends and neighbors, including Jonah Zimles, who has created a wonderful cultural heart to our town in Words

Bookstore, and by the Maplewood Men's Reading Group—we're still going strong a decade in. Tony at Upper Cut, the best-read barber in New Jersey; Jabi and Bozena of Union Pork Store; and the Diamandas family of The Greek Store all keep me trim, fed, and happy. Mozart horn, oboe, and clarinet pieces, Glen Gould's first recording of Bach's *Goldberg Variations*, and, finally, several rounds of first Maria Callas's and then Montserrat Caballe's full recordings of Bellini's opera *Norma* sustained me as I worked. There is nothing like beauty to inspire one to try to create beauty oneself.

Index

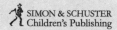

The amazing story of the trapped Chilean miners and their incredible rescue that *Publishers Weekly* calls "a riveting, in-depth recounting of the events that held the world rapt."

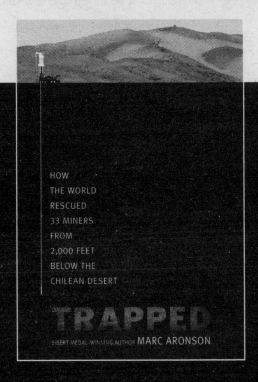

HOW
THE WORLD
RESCUED
33 MINERS
FROM
2,000 FEET
BELOW THE
CHILEAN DESERT

TRAPPED

SIBERT MEDAL-WINNING AUTHOR MARC ARONSON

★"Aronson zips readers through a whirlwind primer. . . . Well-chosen quotes and interviews humanize the headlines, and Aronson's dramatic writing achieves a sense of taut suspense that will captivate young readers."—*Booklist*, starred review

★"Much more than just a chronicle of the Chilean mining disaster of 2010, Aronson's well-researched and riveting book gives readers the sense that they're in the San José copper mine."—*Horn Book*, starred review

"Nonfiction the way it is meant to be—riveting, educational, and entertaining!"—*Library Media Connection*

PRINT AND EBOOK EDITIONS AVAILABLE
From Atheneum Books for Young Readers
athenum   simonandschuster.com/kids

**Irena Sendler has been long forgotten by history.
Until now.**

Adapted for young readers, *Irena's Children* tells the extraordinary story of Irena Sendler, "the female Oskar Schindler," a brave young woman who saved thousands of Jewish children from death and deportation in Nazi-occupied Poland during World War II.

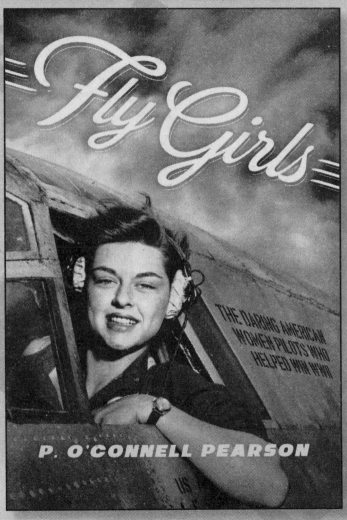